The New March

And a tragic incident

Max Barrington

Max Barrington

Max Barrington

Copyright © 2024 Max Barrington layout design and Copyright © 2024 by MPH Holding Published in 2024 by Etteleah cover and art by MPH Holding

This book is a work of fiction. Unless otherwise indicated, all the names, characters, businesses, places, events and incidents in this book are either the product of the author's imagination or used in a fictitious manner. Any resemblance to actual persons, living or dead, or actual events and/or places is purely coincidental.

All rights reserved. No part of this book may be reproduced or transmitted in any form or by any means, electronic or mechanical, including photocopying, recording, or by information storage and retrieval system, without the author's permission

For the love of my life,
my darling wife and my inspiration,
Lynette

First published in Australia in 2024 by Etteleah Books - Cairns Australia
The New March ISBN 9798323155958

Max Barrington

Max Barrington

Table of Contents

The Bar	1
Fergus Laird	11
Stezland	97
The Muster	159
Restructuring	171
A Plan	199
The Aftermath	223
Epilogue	241
Other Books By Max Barrington	245

Max Barrington

The Bar

It was well over 34°C when Mitchell bought his first beer at the bar of the hotel in Cooktown. It was around one o'clock, and the bar was quiet, with just a dozen or so Aboriginal patrons scattered around. He had just arrived in town and was planning to do some grocery shopping for the housekeeper at the property before heading home. However, as soon as he stepped into the bar, a sudden urge for an icy cold beer took over. The heat was oppressive, and the thought of a refreshing drink was irresistible.

Mitchell had never had a drink at a pub before, as he had only recently turned eighteen. Despite his inexperience with public drinking, he was no stranger to beer itself. Back on his father's property, the accountant had introduced him to the art of brewing. Over time, Mitchell became adept at brewing his own beer, using ingredients shipped all the way from Brisbane. The supplies were collected for him by the accountant from the local freight company in Cooktown. This hobby had given him a sense of pride and a deeper appreciation for the drink he now craved.

It was the first time Mitchell had been into town in nearly three years. The isolation of life on the property meant that trips to Cooktown were few and far between, reserved for essential tasks or special occasions. As he sat at the bar, sipping his beer, he took in his surroundings. The quiet hum of conversation and the faint clinking of glasses created a soothing atmosphere. Outside, the sun blazed relentlessly, but inside the bar, it was cool and calm, a welcome respite from the scorching day.

The New March

Mitchell ordered a stubbie of beer and had drunk about half of it when he placed it on the bar and headed to the men's room. Just as he entered, an Aboriginal man was exiting the room. Without any apparent reason, the man suddenly head butted Mitchell. The unexpected blow sent Mitchell reeling backward, and he fell to the floor, blood streaming from his nose. Dazed and shocked, he tried to process what had just happened, but the man simply walked away as if nothing had occurred.

The girl working behind the bar, witnessing the incident, reacted quickly. With a loud bang, she slammed the roller door above the bar shut, signalling that the bar was temporarily closed. The atmosphere, once quiet and relaxed, turned tense. A few patrons glanced over, but no one approached or intervened.

Mitchell regained his feet, unsteady but determined, and glanced toward the bar. Every Aboriginal male in the room seemed to be watching him closely, their eyes filled with a mixture of curiosity and anticipation, as if waiting to see how he would respond. There were no other white patrons present, and Mitchell suddenly felt very alone. He thought he recognised the man who had struck him, a thickset individual who stood out from the rest. Unlike the slimmer, local Kuku men, this man had the broader build and distinct features of a Kalkadoon, a group Mitchell had learned about in passing.

Pulling a handkerchief from his pocket, Mitchell dabbed at the blood running from his nose, trying to stem the flow that had already left a bright red stain on the front of his freshly laundered khaki shirt. He felt humiliated and angry, emotions swirling in his chest as he wiped his face. Without a word, he turned and walked out of the bar into the oppressive afternoon heat.

He made his way to his 78 Series Landcruiser tray-back utility, unlocked the door, and climbed behind the wheel. For a moment, he just sat there, gripping the steering wheel tightly. His heart was pounding, and his mind raced. He started the engine, but the building rage inside him quickly boiled over. Before he could think better of it, he turned off the motor, threw open the door, and stepped out.

Walking around to the passenger side, he opened the door and reached under the seat, retrieving his Winchester Model 94 .30-30 carbine. His mind was clouded with anger and adrenaline; he wasn't entirely sure what he intended to do, but he knew he wasn't going to let this go unanswered. Gripping the rifle tightly, he marched back toward the hotel, each step fueled by a growing sense of defiance.

As he entered the bar, the atmosphere shifted. The quiet hum of conversation ceased, and all eyes turned to him. A large Aboriginal man, taller and broader than most, approached him cautiously. "What have you there, brother? Don't be silly, bro. Give it here to me," the man said, his voice calm but firm, as he reached out a hand toward Mitchell, seemingly intending to take the rifle.

Mitchell didn't hesitate. In one swift motion, he worked the lever action of the Winchester, sliding one of the five .30-30 150-grain cartridges into the chamber and cocking the rifle. The sound of the action echoed through the bar, sharp and ominous. Without a second thought, he brought the rifle up to his shoulder and fired.

The shot rang out, deafening in the confined space. The man was thrown backward by the force of the impact, landing heavily on the floor. A stunned silence fell over the bar. Mitchell stood there, breathing hard, the rifle still raised, his mind racing to catch up with what had just happened.

The noise from the rifle was shattering, a deafening crack that seemed to echo endlessly through the bar. In that instant, time appeared to stand still. Everyone froze, their eyes fixed on the now lifeless man sprawled on the floor. The metallic scent of gunpowder mingled with the sharp, coppery smell of blood, creating a nauseating atmosphere.

Mitchell, with his rifle still pressed firmly against his shoulder, scanned the room. His eyes locked onto the Kalkadoon man standing at the bar, an expression of shock and disbelief etched across his bearded face. Acting on instinct, Mitchell quickly shifted his aim toward the man's head. In his haste, however, he jerked the trigger rather than applying steady pressure. The resulting shot veered slightly downward, and the heavy .30-30 projectile struck the man in the throat. The force of the impact was devastating, nearly severing his head from his body.

For a brief, harrowing moment, the bar remained in stunned silence. The only sound was the soft, sickening drip of blood pooling onto the wooden floor. Then, a piercing scream shattered the stillness. A woman standing near the decapitated man shrieked in terror as she looked down to see blood spreading rapidly around her feet. Panic seized her, and she bolted across the room toward the side door.

Her movement acted like a starting gun, triggering a chaotic scramble for the exit. Patrons rushed toward the side door, shoving and tripping over one another in their desperation to escape the grisly scene. Chairs clattered to the floor, and glassware shattered as people fought to get out. Meanwhile, another group of men huddled to Mitchell's left, too terrified to move but clearly hoping to slip out through the main door, the same one Mitchell had entered moments earlier.

Mitchell remained standing in the centre of the room, his rifle still raised, his breathing heavy and erratic. His mind was racing, the adrenaline coursing through his veins making it difficult to think clearly. He hadn't planned for this, hadn't anticipated that things would spiral so quickly out of control. And yet, here he was, standing amidst the chaos he had unleashed, with no clear path forward.

The Cooktown police station was situated directly opposite the hotel, a mere 75 meters away. As fate would have it, the local police officer, accompanied by another officer, had just returned to the station and were stepping out of their patrol car when the sharp crack of gunfire pierced the air. Instantly alert, they exchanged a brief, urgent glance. Drawing their Glock 9mm handguns, they sprinted across the street toward the hotel, where they believed the shots had originated.

Reaching the hotel bar, the lead officer pushed through the entrance, arriving just meters behind Mitchell. Adrenaline coursing through his veins, he shouted, "Drop the rifle!" His voice echoed through the chaotic room. Mitchell, disoriented but still on edge, pivoted sharply and, acting on pure instinct, squeezed the trigger. The next round blasted from the Winchester, narrowly missing the officer but tragically striking another man who was halfway through the door behind him. The unfortunate man crumpled to the ground, adding to the mounting horror of the scene.

Reacting swiftly, the officer returned fire, discharging a single shot. The bullet went wide, missing Mitchell entirely. By the time the officer had steadied himself to fire again, Mitchell had already worked the lever action of his rifle. With chilling precision, he aimed and fired at close range. The heavy .30-30 round struck the officer high in the chest, the impact sending him sprawling backward onto the floor.

Meanwhile, the second officer, having entered through the side door amid a flood of panicked patrons, was momentarily overwhelmed by the chaos. As he fought his way through the frightened crowd, he caught sight of his colleague lying motionless on the floor, blood pooling beneath him. Shock froze him in place. His mind struggled to process what he was witnessing, a fellow officer down, the scene in disarray.

Before he could react, Mitchell had already turned his attention toward him. Taking careful aim, Mitchell squeezed the trigger once more. The round struck the officer squarely in the face, the impact dropping him instantly. The bar fell into an eerie silence, broken only by the distant sounds of people fleeing outside and the faint metallic clatter of spent casings hitting the wooden floor.

Breathing heavily, Mitchell surveyed the carnage around him. He lowered his rifle and methodically picked up the four empty casings from the floor, ensuring not to leave any evidence behind. The fifth casing remained lodged in the breach of the Winchester. With a calmness that belied the chaos he had just wrought, Mitchell walked over to the bar. He reached for his half-finished stubbie of beer, took a swig, and carried it with him as he made his way out.

By the time Mitchell had stowed his rifle back under the seat of the Landcruiser and started the engine, the street outside the hotel was eerily deserted. The normally bustling heart of Cooktown now seemed frozen in time, with not a soul in sight. As he drove away, the tension in his chest refused to ease. His mind raced, replaying the events over and over. He couldn't stop thinking, "Why, oh why, did that prick have to do that?" But it was too late for regret. What was done, was done, and now his priority was to get as far away as possible, and fast.

The only route out of Cooktown was via the Mulligan Highway, a long, winding stretch of road that led south to Lakeland. Beyond that, there was a turnoff to the Bloomfield Track, a rough, unsealed route that passed through Wujal Wujal and eventually wound its way into the dense rainforest of the Daintree. The Bloomfield Track was notorious for its challenging road conditions, and depending on the weather, the journey could take up to five hours.

Within an hour of the first reports of the shootings, the police had set up a roadblock on the Mulligan Highway, cutting off the main exit from town. News of the incident had spread quickly, and roadblocks were established at critical points to prevent anyone from leaving the area unnoticed. Mitchell wasn't aware of this yet, but he could feel the pressure mounting. Every minute counted, and he had no choice but to keep moving and hope he could find a way through before the net closed entirely.

The roads leading out of Lakeland offered two main options: one heading north toward Laura and onward to the remote outpost of Weipa, and another heading south toward Mount Carbine. The police, anticipating any potential escape route, had established a roadblock at Laura, effectively cutting off access to the northern Cape York Peninsula. To the south, they had set up another roadblock at Mount Carbine. With these three key roadblocks in place, at Cooktown, Laura, and Mount Carbine, the authorities had effectively sealed off an expansive area of approximately 7,500 square kilometres. They were confident that the individual they sought in connection with the five deaths was still within this perimeter.

Reinforcements were being dispatched from Brisbane and other surrounding regions. Helicopters equipped with thermal imaging, search dogs, and additional tactical units were en route to bolster the search effort. The police believed it was only a matter of time before they apprehended the suspect.

Meanwhile, Mitchell had taken the same route out of Cooktown as he had when he entered earlier that day. He drove west along the Mulligan Highway for 36 kilometres, keeping an eye on his surroundings for any sign of pursuit. At a nondescript turnoff, he veered left onto Kings Plains Road, a rough, unsealed track. The Landcruiser rattled and jolted as he crossed the Annan River, the bridge creaking under the vehicle's weight.

Continuing along the Shiptons Flat Road, he soon reached an unnamed creek spanned by a simple wooden bridge. Instead of crossing over, he made another sharp left turn onto a lesser-known track that led toward a shallow causeway crossing directly through the creek. Water splashed up against the wheels of the Landcruiser as he navigated carefully through the creek, weaving around large boulders, some of which loomed higher than the vehicle itself.

After following the creek bed for nearly a kilometre, Mitchell spotted a familiar rocky outcrop on the left. He guided the Landcruiser up onto a narrow landing between two massive boulders, the tires crunching over loose gravel. From there, he turned right onto a hidden gravel track, a route that only locals familiar with the area would know. The track wound through dense scrubland, offering natural cover from any aerial surveillance. Finally, after several more minutes of cautious driving, the track opened up to reveal his secluded home nestled amidst the thick bushland. It was isolated, difficult to find, and exactly where he needed to be right now.

Fergus Laird

Mitchell's father, Fergus, was the only son of Harris and Olivia Baird. He grew up under a strict and disciplined household on their dairy farm, which neighboured the famous Campbell family property known as Duntroon. This historic estate would later become the Royal Military College Duntroon, cementing its place in Australian military history.

Fergus' upbringing was rigid, with little room for personal freedom. By the time he completed his higher school certificate, he had been hoping to take a 'gap' year to experience life beyond the farm and academics. However, his father, Harris, was adamant that there would be no such indulgence. Instead, Fergus was promptly enrolled at the Australian National University, where he studied civil engineering. In 1962, at the age of 22, he successfully earned his degree.

Despite his personal aspirations, Fergus found himself once again under the influence of his father's firm expectations. Following strong insistence from Harris, Fergus enrolled as a cadet at the Royal Military College, Duntroon. His engineering qualifications accelerated his progress through the program, and within 18 months, he graduated as a Lieutenant Specialist Service Officer. He was subsequently attached to the Royal Australian Engineers, a branch that would come to define much of his professional life.

In 1965, Fergus was deployed to Vietnam, where he served with distinction as part of 3 Troop, 1 Field Squadron, Royal Australian Engineers. This unit would later earn the nickname 'The Tunnel Rats,' renowned for their dangerous and highly specialised work clearing and navigating the extensive tunnel networks used by the VietCong. Fergus served three tours in Vietnam, during which he honed his skills in jungle warfare, explosives, and field engineering. His experience and leadership earned him the respect of his men, but his strict adherence to discipline, a trait deeply ingrained by his father, also created friction with some of his subordinates.

After a decade of service, Fergus left the army in 1975, having risen to the rank of Major. His departure marked the end of a significant chapter in his life. He left behind many close friends forged in the crucible of war, but he also left behind enemies, those who had chafed under his rigid command style.

Both Fergus's mother and father were tragically killed in a car accident on the Monaro Highway later that same year while on their way to the New South Wales snowfields for a skiing holiday. The loss of his mother was a crushing blow for Fergus, but the passing of his father did not evoke the same depth of grief. With his parents gone, Fergus inherited the family property, which he promptly sold to the Federal Government. The sale made him enormously wealthy, giving him the financial freedom to take a year-long holiday in Scotland, the land of his parents' ancestry.

During his time in Scotland, Fergus met a young woman named Amelia in Ayrshire. The two quickly fell in love, and they married shortly thereafter. In 1978, Fergus and Amelia returned to Cairns, Queensland, where they settled on a small property in the picturesque Little Mulgrave Valley.

Two years later, in 1980, Amelia gave birth to their only son, Mitchell Harris Baird.

Amelia adored Mitchell, doting on him constantly and ensuring that he had everything he desired, whether it was necessary or not. She believed he could do no wrong and indulged his every whim. As a result, Mitchell developed a strong sense of entitlement. If denied what he wanted, he would throw intense tantrums, a trait Amelia often excused as being inherited from Fergus, who was known for his own foul temper when things didn't go his way.

When Mitchell reached school age, Amelia took on the role of his devoted chauffeur, driving him to school each morning and picking him up each afternoon. She remained deeply involved in his daily life, shielding him from difficulties and ensuring that he was always comfortable. This overprotectiveness would later shape Mitchell's personality, fostering both his confidence and his inability to cope with setbacks.

Mitchell was only ten years old when a tragic accident changed his life forever. He had accompanied his mother on a routine shopping trip to Cairns, a journey that should have been uneventful. As they drove along the highway at the speed limit of one hundred kilometres per hour, a police car that had just finished booking another driver suddenly sped off and cut in front of them without warning. Amelia, Mitchell's mother, swerved sharply to the right in an attempt to avoid a collision, but in doing so, she lost control of the vehicle. Their car veered off the road and crashed into a tree, resulting in a catastrophic accident that instantly claimed Amelia's life.

Although Mitchell had been a direct witness to the entire incident and could clearly describe what had happened, the police quickly placed the blame on his deceased mother. Mitchell tried to explain how the police car's reckless driving had forced his mother off the road, but no one seemed interested in hearing his account. The officers dismissed his testimony with a wave of indifference, saying, "He's just a ten-year-old kid."

To further complicate matters, the officer involved claimed that he had still been engaged with the driver he had pulled over when the accident occurred. He denied any involvement in the incident, asserting that Amelia had simply lost control of her vehicle on her own. Adding to the injustice, the officer's notebook, which supposedly contained the details of the driver he had stopped, mysteriously disappeared. Without that key piece of evidence, there was no way to corroborate Mitchell's version of events or hold the officer accountable.

The accident and its aftermath left Mitchell deeply scarred. Not only had he lost his mother, but he had also experienced firsthand the indifference and failure of those in authority. This incident would plant the seeds of a deep-seated mistrust in the police, a sentiment that would grow stronger as he grew older.

Following the death of his wife, Fergus became increasingly withdrawn from society. Once a disciplined and driven man, he now harbored a deep-seated resentment toward the police and, more broadly, toward anyone outside of his immediate world. The only exception to this bitterness was his son, Mitchell, who was himself adrift in a sea of confusion and grief after losing his mother. Mitchell's world had been turned upside down; the comforting certainty of always getting what he wanted was gone, replaced by a harsh new reality he could neither understand nor control.

Mitchell struggled to comprehend the lies he had been told by the police. He had clearly seen the police car pull out in front of them with his own eyes, and he couldn't fathom why the officer had denied being behind the wheel at the time of the accident. Even more bewildering was the behaviour of the other officers who questioned him. Rather than seeking the truth, they accused Mitchell of lying and threatened him with imprisonment if he continued to insist that the police officer had caused the accident. The experience left him deeply shaken.

These events planted a bitter seed in Mitchell's heart. The betrayal by the very people who were supposed to serve and protect created a sense of disillusionment that would stay with him for years to come. He knew, from that moment on, that he could never trust the police again. As the weeks turned into months, the bond between Fergus and Mitchell grew stronger, forged by shared grief and a mutual distrust of authority. Together, they navigated a world that now felt alien and hostile, each quietly carrying the scars of that fateful day.

On the day of his mother's funeral at Saint Monica's Church in Cairns City, Fergus booked a room for himself and Mitchell at the Cairns International Hotel, conveniently located within walking distance of the church. The funeral had been emotionally draining, and later that night, Fergus left Mitchell in the company of some family friends who were also staying at the hotel. Grief-stricken and craving solitude, Fergus slipped away from the group. He was overwhelmed by the weight of his loss and sought solace in solitude, perhaps with the numbing comfort of alcohol.

Crossing the street to the Great Northern Hotel, Fergus purchased a bottle of Johnny Walker Scotch whisky. With the bottle in hand, he wandered down to a quiet, empty bench on the Esplanade, far from the bustling streets, where he could grieve in peace. Sitting there, gazing out over the dark water, he raised the bottle in a quiet, tearful toast to his late wife, his heart aching with sorrow.

His moment of mourning, however, was brutally interrupted when three Aboriginal men approached him. They jeered at him, shouting that he was "white shit" and demanding that he leave their land. One of them, a squat man with a broad, bearded face, snatched the bottle of whisky from Fergus, spilling its contents onto the ground. The loss of the whisky was the least of Fergus's concerns; the situation rapidly escalated as the other two men squared up to attack him.

For what felt like an eternity, the two men pummelled Fergus with their fists. He staggered under the blows, his mind flashing back to the battlefields of Vietnam, where survival often depended on quick reflexes and brutal efficiency. As the squat man raised the empty whisky bottle to strike him, Fergus reacted instinctively. His training took over. With a swift, calculated motion, he delivered a sharp chop with the edge of his hand across the bridge of the assailant's nose, instantly breaking the bone. Without hesitation, he followed up with an upward thrust of the heel of his other hand, driving the broken bone into the man's brain. The man collapsed lifelessly to the ground.

Before Fergus could fully regain his balance, one of the remaining attackers picked up the fallen bottle and smashed it down onto the top of Fergus's head with full force. The bottle shattered on impact, slicing through his scalp and leaving deep lacerations. Blood poured from the wound as Fergus crumpled to the ground, dazed and disoriented, the world around him spinning into darkness.

Fergus awoke in the Cairns Hospital sometime during the following afternoon, groggy and disoriented, only to learn that he had sustained a fractured skull, three broken ribs, and multiple lacerations. What shocked him even more was the news that he was under arrest for murder and would be taken into custody immediately upon his discharge from the hospital, scheduled in approximately three days. The attending nurse, responding to his urgent request, arranged for a telephone to be connected by his bedside. Fergus wasted no time and called his longtime friend and solicitor, Brian Haptu, explaining his dire predicament and asking for legal advice.

Brian arrived at the hospital later that evening, grim-faced but composed. He reassured Fergus that he would do everything possible to help, though the situation was complicated. "It doesn't look good, Fergus," Brian admitted. "They're pushing hard for a murder conviction, and the Aboriginal Legal Service is well-funded. They'll bring in some of the top Queen's Counsel barristers. We'll have to fight tooth and nail."

On the day of his discharge, Fergus appeared in court, where he was formally charged with murder. However, given his standing as a respected Cairns citizen and the minimal risk of flight, he was granted bail. He now had roughly three months to prepare for his trial, though the path ahead seemed grim. Brian had warned him that, regardless of the final verdict, jail time was almost inevitable, even though he had acted in self-defence. The reality was harsh: the legal system appeared poised to make an example of him.

Over the next few weeks, Brian worked tirelessly on Fergus's case, seeking the best possible defence. The strategy was to plead guilty to manslaughter, hoping to avoid a harsher sentence for murder. Meanwhile, Fergus signed over power of attorney to Brian to manage his financial and personal affairs during his likely incarceration. To ensure that Mitchell would be taken care of, Fergus arranged for him to attend St. Augustine's College as a boarding student. Though reluctant to be separated from his son, Fergus knew he had no choice; Mitchell's well-being was his top priority.

Despite Brian's efforts, including the hiring of the highly esteemed Sir James Whitby QC to lead the defence, the outcome was sobering. After an intense legal battle, Fergus was sentenced to seven years in prison, with eligibility for parole after five. The courtroom felt heavy and oppressive as the sentence was read out, Fergus's mind reeling with disbelief. All he could think was, Is this justice? He had fought for this country, served with honour, and now, after defending himself in an unprovoked attack, he was being sent to prison.

As he left the courtroom in the custody of officers, Fergus couldn't help but feel a deep sense of betrayal. He had risked his life for the ideals of a nation he no longer recognised. The legal system, once something he had respected, now seemed indifferent to the complexities of real-life situations. He was no longer just a citizen but a convict, and the thought of being away from his son for so many years filled him with dread. All he could do was hope that Brian would help Mitchell navigate the challenges ahead, ensuring that his son's future remained bright, even as his own life descended into darkness.

Thus began a long, painful chapter in Fergus's life, one filled with regret, disillusionment, and an ever-growing resentment toward the country he had once proudly served.

Mitchell hated the boarding school from the moment he arrived. It wasn't just the unfamiliar environment, it was the profound absence of everything that had ever made him feel safe. He missed his home, but even more, he missed his mother. Each night, as he lay in his cold, unfamiliar bed, he silently cried himself to sleep, longing for her comforting presence. The warmth of her voice, her reassuring smile, those were now only distant memories, and he was left to confront an overwhelming sense of loneliness.

Mitchell's isolation at school was almost inevitable. Having grown up sheltered and pampered by his mother, he had little in common with the other boys. His childhood had been marked by restrictions meant to protect him, no football because it was too dangerous, no horse because he might fall, no sleepovers because other children were deemed too rough and unruly. Now, in this new environment, he found himself unprepared for the rough camaraderie of his peers. He lacked the social skills to integrate and quickly became an outsider.

At boarding school, there was no one to shield him. He had to fend for himself, and over time, he disciplined himself to rely on no one. He resolved to get through each day on his own terms, counting down the days until his father would return and take him home. Even though home wasn't the same without his mother, it was still better than the cold, regimented world of boarding school.

It didn't take long for the other boys to learn that Mitchell wasn't someone to mess with lightly. While he didn't seek out conflict, he was quick to retaliate when provoked. One particular incident cemented his reputation. While Mitchell was sitting in a toilet stall, a boy decided to play a cruel prank by reaching under the cubicle door with a gas cigarette lighter and setting fire to the cuffs of Mitchell's trousers. Mitchell had managed to extinguish the flames, but he was furious. His anger wasn't just about the prank, it was the culmination of weeks of frustration, isolation, and helplessness.

Determined to send a clear message, Mitchell waited for the right moment to retaliate. A few days later, he spotted the same boy entering a toilet cubicle. Armed with a can of WD-40 and an extension tube attached to the nozzle, he crouched outside the stall and began spraying the flammable liquid under the door. With the flick of a gas lighter, he ignited the spray. The resulting explosion was small but powerful enough to startle the boy and cause minor burns, landing him in the hospital.

The incident sent shockwaves through the school. The staff launched an immediate investigation, and Mitchell was summoned before the headmaster. Despite the seriousness of the situation, Mitchell remained calm and unyielding. He didn't offer any excuses or apologies, and though he didn't openly admit to the act, it was clear he had no regrets. The headmaster, faced with a boy who was clearly troubled but also fiercely independent, decided against expulsion. Instead, Mitchell was put on probation and assigned mandatory counselling sessions, though it was doubtful anyone could truly reach him.

Word of the incident spread quickly among the students, and from that point on, most of them either avoided Mitchell altogether or treated him with wary respect. He had become something of a legend, quiet, distant, but dangerously capable when pushed too far. Despite his growing reputation, Mitchell remained a loner. He didn't crave friendship or approval; he simply wanted to endure the experience until the day he could leave.

Though Mitchell's actions earned him a degree of respect, they also marked a turning point. The once-quiet, pampered boy had hardened. The world had already taken so much from him, his mother, his home, and now his childhood. In response, Mitchell built walls around himself, determined never to let anyone hurt him again.

Although it seemed that every student at the school was aware of who was responsible for the explosion, no one was reprimanded. The situation was complicated by the fact that it was widely accepted as common knowledge among the student body that Mitchell was a particularly vengeful individual, known for settling scores in unusual and often elaborate ways. This reputation only grew more solid when, for reasons unknown, one of the teachers had slapped Mitchell across the face. Though corporal punishment was not uncommon in the school, this particular incident had a far more severe outcome than anyone had anticipated. The slap caused Mitchell's nose to bleed so heavily that he had to be rushed to the hospital, where doctors worked frantically to stop the relentless flow of blood.

The aftermath of the incident was swift, yet the staff seemed to remain blissfully ignorant of the threat that Mitchell posed. Only a day later, the same teacher who had struck Mitchell was in for an unpleasant surprise. After starting his Subaru motor car in the school car park, there was a sudden and deafening bang that reverberated through the area. The car, once a reliable commuter vehicle, was now in critical condition, as both of its head gaskets had blown completely. A costly repair job was imminent.

When the garage workers inspected the car, they discovered something unusual: a large potato had been shoved entirely over the exhaust pipe. The outer skin of the potato had been meticulously peeled away, leaving only the interior to sit inside the exhaust system, making it nearly impossible to detect. When the engine was started, the back pressure from the exhaust system had been too much for the gaskets to handle, and they had blown under the strain. The garage's findings made it clear to anyone familiar with Mitchell's capabilities that this was not an accident. It was a calculated act of retaliation.

The staff knew who the culprit was, of course, but as there was no direct evidence linking Mitchell to the incident, they could do nothing. Mitchell had once again displayed his knack for revenge in a way that was impossible to prove, leaving both the teacher and the school with no recourse but to silently acknowledge the truth. Though it was widely understood that Mitchell had orchestrated the sabotage, there was no way to hold him accountable, and life at the school carried on, its undercurrents of tension and unspoken threats only deepening.

It was 1993 when Fergus was released from prison, and by then, Mitchell had grown into a fifteen-year-old on the cusp of adulthood. He was looking forward to the idea of completing his studies at Gordonvale High School and then returning home to resume a normal life. But that dream was abruptly shattered when his father, Fergus, announced that he was selling the Little Mulgrave property and relocating north to Cooktown. Mitchell's heart sank as he was informed that he would be joining his father up there once he had finished his education at St Augustine's. There was, however, a small consolation; Mitchell would be able to spend his holidays up north with Fergus. Still, that wasn't enough to ease the overwhelming sense of abandonment Mitchell now felt. The bond that he and his father had once shared seemed to fray and unravel with every word Fergus spoke. Mitchell felt rejected, cast aside, and left behind in a way he never expected. The idea of starting over, far from his friends and the life he had known, filled him with resentment and unease.

While Fergus had been in prison, he had forged an unlikely friendship with an elderly inmate named Stephen Murray, though everyone simply called him 'Stez.' Stez had quickly become a guiding figure for Fergus during his time behind bars. The two had grown close, eventually becoming cellmates. Stez, with his wisdom and years of experience, taught Fergus how to navigate the harsh realities of prison life, showing him whom to trust and whom to avoid. He offered advice on how to survive, not just physically but mentally, in an environment designed to break people down.

Stez hailed from Shiptons Flat, a remote and rugged area near Cooktown. He'd been born at the Cooktown Hospital, though Stez himself was quick to joke that it was more a "building with a bed" than a real hospital. His father had tried his hand at grazing in the region, but the harsh conditions, including frequent crocodile attacks and raids by local Aborigines, had wiped out most of the cattle. Undeterred, Stez's father had also invested in gold mining. The area had been rich in minerals, tin, wolfram, and gold, but many of the mines had been difficult to work, and some had gone under. Still, Stez spoke fondly of the region, recounting tales of his father's perseverance.

Over the years, Stez had inherited a substantial property, much of it consisting of leased land with mineral deposits, but some portions of his land were freehold, making it a valuable asset. His holdings stretched over 110,000 acres, from Shiptons Flat to Cedar Bay, and further down to Wujal Wujal and the Bloomfield River. The land was diverse, ranging from dense, lush rainforests to lighter, more open timbered areas with scattered clearings and scrubland. There were a number of old mines scattered throughout the property, and Stez had invested in acquiring land from miners and farmers who couldn't make a success of it.

However, Stez had been suffering from a serious illness for the last few years of Fergus's sentence, and just before Fergus was released, Stez passed away. The loss of Stez hit Fergus harder than he expected. Over the years, Stez had become more than just a fellow inmate; he had been a mentor, a friend, and a source of stability in a place where everything else felt uncertain. The grief was profound, but it would pale in comparison to the shock Fergus would experience upon learning of Stez's final wishes.

In his will, Stez had left everything he owned to Fergus, including his prized 110,000 acres of land at Shiptons Flat. It was a vast and wild property, far beyond anything Fergus had ever imagined owning, and now it was his to explore.

The inheritance seemed almost surreal, a twist of fate that was both overwhelming and exhilarating. Fergus had always dreamed of a fresh start, and now, with Stez's death, he was presented with an opportunity to create a new life in a place that held both mystery and promise.

As Fergus prepared to explore his new property, he couldn't help but reflect on the twists of fate that had brought him to this point. The loss of his father's land, the relationship he had with Mitchell growing strained, and now this unexpected inheritance. The land at Shiptons Flat was more than just a piece of property, it was a symbol of a new chapter, one that would require Fergus to navigate not only the rugged wilderness of his new land but the complexities of his fractured relationships as well.

Fergus was determined to make the most of his inheritance, and he threw himself into gathering every bit of information he could about his new property. He had obtained a collection of council plans, boundary maps, and topographical charts of the area, hoping to get a full understanding of what he had inherited. He had also carefully studied the lay of the land, piecing together as much as possible about the geography, the location of buildings, and the various features that made up what he had come to refer to as "Stezland." The name, though informal, seemed fitting for the vast expanse of land that Stez had left to him. It was an area full of untapped potential, with rugged terrain and a history steeped in both natural beauty and human toil.

For Fergus's first visit to Stezland, he knew he needed to take someone along to help with the exploration, and who better than Mitchell? The decision seemed almost natural, considering that the long weekend was approaching. It would be the perfect opportunity for father and son to venture into the unknown together. Fergus had planned a full weekend of daytime reconnaissance, which would give them a chance to cover a significant portion of the property. To make things comfortable, they would stay in a motel in Cooktown, which was a mere forty-five kilometres away from Shiptons Flat. It was a manageable distance, giving them the perfect balance between exploration and rest.

In preparation for the trip, Fergus had recently purchased a new Land Rover Defender 90 TDI, a rugged and reliable vehicle that he thought would be ideal for navigating the rough terrain of Stezland. The Defender's high clearance, four-wheel drive capability, and off-road prowess made it the perfect choice for the kind of exploration he anticipated. Fergus could already picture himself driving through the dense undergrowth, the powerful engine humming as they ventured deeper into the wilderness. It wasn't just a practical choice, it was also a symbol of a new beginning for him, a vehicle that would carry him through the untamed beauty of the land he was now responsible for.

As he studied the maps and plans, Fergus noted that there were multiple buildings scattered throughout the property. One of the most significant structures was the main house, which was located just across an unnamed creek. The house itself had been left untouched for a long time. Stez had been imprisoned for twelve years, and Fergus had known him for at least four of those years. This meant that the property, and specifically the main house, had been abandoned for at least sixteen years. The thought of stepping into that house filled Fergus with a sense of anticipation. What had it been like when Stez had lived there? What had the house become after so many years of neglect?

Fergus couldn't help but feel a sense of curiosity mixed with excitement as he imagined what awaited them. The house had probably deteriorated over the years, but perhaps there were still remnants of Stez's life and legacy within its walls. Whether it was the furniture, personal items, or just the atmosphere of the place, Fergus was eager to uncover what had been left behind. He knew the land would offer him a fresh start, but this house, abandoned and untouched for so long, held a connection to the past that he couldn't ignore. It was more than just a building; it was a link to Stez, to a friendship that had profoundly impacted Fergus during his years in prison.

The long weekend couldn't come soon enough. As Fergus made his preparations, he couldn't shake the feeling that this trip would mark the beginning of something pivotal in his life, a journey into both the land that had been left to him and the unresolved complexities of his own relationships, particularly with Mitchell. The exploration of Stezland was not just a physical journey; it was the start of an emotional and personal odyssey that Fergus wasn't entirely sure he was ready for, but one he would have to undertake nonetheless.

On the Friday before the long weekend, Fergus had everything packed and ready for the trip to Cooktown. He had been looking forward to this journey for some time, an exploration of both the land Stez had left him and the uncharted territory of his own future. The drive was going to be an important bonding experience for him and Mitch, or "Mitch" as he now preferred to be called, ever since he had started to assert his independence in those teenage years. Fergus picked him up from college, and together they set off for Cooktown, the town where the adventure would begin.

As they drove along the winding roads, Fergus found himself talking about Stez, reminiscing about their time together in prison, the bond they had forged, and how Stez had helped him survive those gruelling years. He spoke with admiration for his old friend, emphasising the invaluable role Stez had played in helping him adjust to the harsh realities of prison life. Over the years, Stez had shown him the ropes, teaching him who to trust and how to navigate the dangerous and unpredictable world of incarceration. When Fergus mentioned that Stez had left him the vast property at Shiptons Flat, Mitch was taken aback.

"You're joking, Dad?" Mitch asked, his voice laced with disbelief.

Fergus chuckled at Mitch's reaction, understanding how hard it was to believe. "Hard to believe, isn't it? God knows what it may be worth now, and god knows what we'll find when we get there," he said, a hint of both excitement and uncertainty in his tone.

There was a pause, and then Mitch asked, "What was this guy, Stez, in prison for, Dad?"

Fergus's face tightened slightly, the question digging at a memory he had never fully understood. "I have no idea, Mitch. He would never tell me. I asked him countless times, but he never said a word. I respected that, though, sometimes you just don't ask about things like that."

Mitch nodded, taking in the silence that followed, both of them contemplating the mystery of Stez's past. It was a subject Fergus had never pushed. Whatever Stez had done to land in prison, it wasn't something that mattered in the end. What mattered now was that Stez had left behind something valuable, something that could change Fergus's life, and Mitch's, too, if they could make something of it.

Fergus chose to take the inland route to Cooktown, mindful of the weather. There had been a lot of rain recently, and with king tides running, the Bloomfield River crossing could be tricky. There was the possibility of a long wait if the river was too high, and he didn't want to waste time standing around, so the inland route was the safer option. The road was quieter, and the journey felt more remote, with only the sound of tires against wet asphalt and the occasional rumble of thunder breaking the silence.

When they finally reached Cooktown, it was around 7:30 PM. The drive had taken longer than expected due to heavy traffic as holidaymakers flocked to the area for the weekend. It seemed that everyone had the same idea, and the congestion slowed them down significantly. Fergus wasn't bothered by the delay, though, it gave him more time to talk to Mitch, to try to connect before the next part of their journey.

The motel they checked into had a beautiful view overlooking the Coral Sea. The sound of the waves crashing against the shore offered a relaxing backdrop to their arrival. But their relief was short-lived. When they went to the motel's restaurant, they found it fully booked, likely due to the influx of weekend tourists. Undeterred, they decided to walk the short distance to the RSL club, hoping to find a good meal there. It turned out to be a great choice, and they enjoyed a satisfying dinner in the welcoming atmosphere of the club.

But their evening took an unpleasant turn when they returned to the motel. As they walked back, they were approached by a group of Aborigines, first asking for cigarettes. When Fergus politely told them they didn't have any, the request shifted to money. When Fergus informed them that they didn't have any cash on hand either, the tone of the interaction changed drastically.

The group grew hostile, their language vulgar and abusive. They yelled at them, demanding that they "get out of our country," their words laced with contempt. Fergus's temper flared. He had spent years in prison, and the thought of being intimidated or belittled by anyone, especially in such a disrespectful manner, was something he could not tolerate.

Mitch could see his father's fists clench, his body tense with barely contained fury. Fergus had always kept a tight grip on his anger, but in that moment, it was clear he was ready to act. The thought flashed through his mind, if Mitch hadn't been with him, he would've made sure those men learned the hard way not to cross him. But he bit back the impulse, knowing that Mitch's presence was the one thing keeping him in check.

"Let's just get inside," Fergus muttered, his voice low and tight with restraint.

Mitch could feel the tension radiating from his father, and though he didn't fully understand what had caused the violent outburst, he sensed that his father was a man with a past, one that didn't easily let go of old habits. The rest of the walk to the motel was in silence, the weight of the encounter hanging over them both. For Fergus, it was a reminder of the harshness of life, of the rage that still simmered beneath the surface, a reminder that, no matter where he went, some battles were harder to avoid than others.

Saturday morning arrived with the promise of adventure. As Fergus and Mitch made their way to Shiptons Flat, the excitement of exploring Stezland was palpable in the air. Fergus was driving the newly purchased Land Rover Defender 90 TDI, and he couldn't help but feel a certain pride in his choice of vehicle. It was rugged, reliable, and perfect for navigating the terrain of the property he now owned. The Land Rover's powerful engine hummed steadily beneath him, its suspension absorbing the bumps and dips of the dirt roads with ease. He was genuinely impressed with the vehicle, which performed well on the rough roads leading to their destination.

Mitch, however, was less than impressed. "Dad," he remarked, eyeing the vehicle with a dismissive smirk, "these types of vehicles are regarded as 'poufter' four-wheel drives.

If you want real off-road power, a Landcruiser is the only way to go."

Fergus raised an eyebrow but didn't rise to the bait. "Is that right?" was all he said, his voice calm and measured. "We'll see."

Despite Mitch's teasing, the two of them fell into an easy rhythm as they continued their journey. Mitch was navigating, glancing at the map and calling out directions. The route to Shiptons Flat was relatively straightforward at first, with the first major landmark being the Annan River, which they crossed without issue. After that, there was another bridge over an unnamed creek, and then they would need to find a track on the right in about six kilometres.

But when they reached the designated distance, they found no track. Mitch double-checked the map, but there was nothing to suggest they had missed it. They decided to continue for another three kilometres, hoping to find the elusive track. Just when they were about to lose hope, Fergus spotted a faint track to the right. He slowed the Land Rover and came to a stop, staring at the map intently. He examined both the council boundary maps and the topographical map, confirming that this track appeared to be part of their land, Stezland.

"Well, we're going this way," Fergus said, making a decision with quiet confidence.

Mitch glanced at the map, nodding in agreement, though he had his doubts. They followed the track for about two kilometres, navigating through the dense bush and the uneven ground. The track was rough, but the Land Rover handled it well, the wheels gripping the dirt and gravel with ease.

Eventually, they came upon another track branching off to the right. Both Fergus and Mitch assumed this was the track that had been marked on the map but was missing earlier. They decided to follow it, eager to see where it would lead. After a few minutes of driving, the dense foliage began to clear, revealing an open space, a small clearing. In the distance, they could make out the silhouette of a house.

As they drew closer, they saw a thin wisp of smoke curling up from behind the house, suggesting someone was using a fire, perhaps cooking or keeping warm. Fergus felt a mix of curiosity and caution. The house, however, looked worn and weathered, as though it had seen much better days. It seemed abandoned, but the smoke hinted that maybe it wasn't.

Fergus brought the Land Rover to a stop and got out of the vehicle, taking a deep breath as he surveyed the area. He reached into the car and pulled out the council boundary map, as well as the topographical map, which he laid out on the bonnet of the car to compare the information. He carefully examined both maps, confirming the location.

He pointed to the boundary lines on the council map, then traced his finger across the topographical map. "We're definitely on Stezland," he said, his voice filled with certainty.

Mitch leaned over to get a closer look, and after studying the maps for a moment, he nodded. "No doubt about it, Dad. This is our land."

But the discovery raised more questions than answers. If this house was on their land, then why was someone living there? Fergus's mind raced as he tried to make sense of the situation. According to the maps and council drawings, there was another homestead located about seven kilometres north of this one. The presence of someone living here, so close to the main house, was strange, and it suggested that Stez's property had either been inhabited by squatters or perhaps leased to someone else over the years.

"Looks like someone's been using the place," Fergus muttered, mostly to himself. "But who?"

Mitch seemed uneasy, glancing at the house from the window of the Land Rover. "Should we go up there?" he asked cautiously, unsure of what to expect.

Fergus hesitated. He knew they needed to find out what was going on with the house, but at the same time, he didn't want to rush into a potentially awkward or even confrontational situation. The house, though abandoned in appearance, might hold some clues about Stez's legacy. "Let's just take a look, but we'll keep our distance for now," Fergus decided.

With that, they slowly drove closer, making sure to keep a respectful distance from the house as they continued their exploration of the land. The wheels of the Land Rover crunched the gravel as they crept forward, and both father and son sat in silence, their minds racing with questions about the strange house ahead, and about the mysteries Stezland held in store for them.

They drove slowly up to the house, the rough track leading them to a dilapidated structure that seemed to have been abandoned for years. The house was a far cry from what Fergus had imagined when he'd first set his sights on Stezland. The paint was peeling, the roof sagging in places, and weeds had taken over the small yard, overtaking the path that once might have led to the front door. A few stray boards were nailed haphazardly to the sides, likely as a makeshift attempt to keep the place from falling apart altogether.

Out front, there was an old Nissan four-wheel-drive ute parked near the porch, its paint faded and worn by the relentless sun. A rusty truck sat off to the side, its wheels half-sunk in the dry earth. As they pulled up, two dogs came charging out of the yard, barking furiously. Their approach was aggressive, and they didn't seem particularly friendly.

Fergus, however, was unfazed. He glanced at Mitch, who was still sitting in the passenger seat, and gave him a quiet, reassuring nod. "Stay in the car, Mitch. I'll handle this," he instructed.

Without another word, Fergus stepped out of the Land Rover. The dogs immediately intensified their barking, their fur bristling as they closed in on him. But Fergus didn't flinch. He walked with a steady, confident pace, ignoring the growling and snapping of the dogs. They hesitated for a moment, sensing that this man wasn't afraid. The change was almost instant. The dogs' aggression seemed to wane, and they started to quiet down, cautiously sniffing the air around him, trying to gauge who he was.

Before long, the door to the house creaked open, and a man stepped out onto the porch. He was of average height with unkempt dark hair, a scruffy, patchy beard that looked like it hadn't seen a razor in months, and his clothes were ragged, torn jeans and a faded khaki shirt, possibly from some military surplus store. His overall appearance was one of neglect, a person who had spent too much time on the fringes of society.

The man didn't greet Fergus with a smile. Instead, he squinted at him from the porch, his expression cautious but not entirely hostile. "Hello," he called out, his voice rough and unwelcoming. "Are you guys looking for something?"

Fergus didn't immediately respond with a direct answer. He studied the man carefully, noting the slight edge in his voice and the guarded posture. "We're just having a look around," Fergus replied evenly, maintaining an air of calm.

The man's demeanour changed slightly, his brow furrowing. "Well, don't go looking too far," he warned. "You're on private property."

"Oh, is this your property?" Fergus asked, his interest piqued now. Something about the man's attitude was odd, and Fergus couldn't shake the feeling that there was more to the situation than met the eye.

The man didn't seem to appreciate the question. His eyes narrowed, and he shifted his weight, crossing his arms. "No," he snapped. "Not that it's any of your business, but I'm the caretaker for the owner."

Fergus's curiosity grew stronger. He had suspected as much, but now the confirmation piqued his interest even more. He took a step forward, hoping to press for more information. "Do you know the owner?" he asked. "Does he live around here?"

As he spoke, Fergus noticed a movement inside the house, someone peering through the side curtain, watching the conversation unfold. The figure remained hidden, but it was clear they were paying attention.

The caretaker's face tightened at the question, his eyes flicking to the window where the figure had been. He was growing more agitated now. "Why?" he asked, his tone defensive. "Do you want him for something?"

Fergus stayed calm, but the sharpness in his voice became more evident. "Yes," he replied. "I'd like to know who he is and how I can contact him. It's quite important, actually."

The man hesitated, his gaze flickering back to the house, as if considering whether or not to offer more information. But after a tense moment, he crossed his arms tighter and let out an annoyed sigh. "Well, he's away in Cairns just now," he said brusquely, as if dismissing the topic entirely. "And he can't be contacted, so it might be a good idea if you just get off the property now."

Fergus could sense the man's growing irritation, but he knew better than to react rashly. He wasn't about to let this go without more information, but he also didn't want to escalate things. The caretaker was clearly on edge, and it wasn't lost on Fergus that there was someone inside the house, potentially watching the exchange with interest. The last thing he wanted was a confrontation, especially if the person inside the house was armed.

"Alright, I hear you," Fergus said, taking a step back. His mind was racing, though. He needed to find out more. Who was this caretaker? Who was the owner of the property?

And what was really going on at this house? Everything about the situation seemed off.

He turned to walk back toward the Land Rover, motioning for Mitch to stay put. But just as he reached the car, he heard the caretaker call out again.

"You'd better leave now," the man shouted, his voice edging toward a growl. "Before I call the cops."

"This might come as a surprise to you, but I am the rightful owner of this property. The transfer was completed two months ago, and frankly, I think you're lying," Fergus said, his tone firm and unwavering. The man stood frozen, his gaze fixed blankly on Fergus as if trying to process the information.

Fergus opened the back door of the Land Rover, retrieved a folder, and pulled out the council documents, including copies of the titles and boundary plans. With a deliberate motion, he placed the documents on the bonnet of the vehicle, his eyes never leaving the man.

"Take a look," Fergus said, his voice cool and authoritative. "Come over here. These papers confirm everything."

Reluctantly, the man began to walk towards the Land Rover. As he approached, Fergus turned to face him fully, extending his right arm in a firm handshake. "I'm Fergus Baird," he said, his tone not leaving room for dispute. "And this is my son, Mitchell."

The man hesitated for a moment, then slowly shook Fergus' hand. His face was still a mix of confusion and disbelief, but he nodded toward Mitchell in the car without saying anything.

"Rodney Hadrick," the man finally muttered, his voice trailing off. "And this is Jason," he added, gesturing to another figure emerging from the house.

Fergus held his ground, still watching Rodney closely, sensing the shift in the man's demeanour. There was no turning back now. "I think it's time we have a proper conversation."

Rodney, now appearing somewhat more at ease, suggested they come inside. "I'll make you a cup of coffee," he offered, though it was clear from his tone that he wasn't particularly enthusiastic about the idea. Fergus politely declined the coffee but accepted the invitation to step inside.

To his surprise, the inside of the house was far tidier and more orderly than he had expected. They moved into the kitchen, where a large, handmade table stood, crafted from local hardwood. It was neat and well-maintained, and the overall atmosphere was much more inviting than Fergus had imagined.

Jason, noticing Mitchell's presence, asked with a smile, "Would you like a Coke, mate?"

Mitchell nodded, a small smile forming on his face. "Yeah, that'd be great."

"Coming right up," Jason replied, opening a slightly outdated fridge, but one that appeared fully functional. As he handed Mitchell a cold can of Coke, he looked over at Fergus. "Too early for a beer?" Jason asked, a hint of playfulness in his voice.

Fergus chuckled, shaking his head. "Why not? If everyone else is having one, I'll join in."

"Make it three," Rodney added, settling himself at the table, his demeanour shifting to a more relaxed tone as he gestured for Fergus to sit down.

The air between them seemed to soften, though Fergus remained keenly aware that there were still many questions left unanswered. As they settled into the conversation, the sound of a vehicle pulling up outside caught Fergus' attention.

"That'll be the missus and Jas's girlfriend," Rodney said, standing up briefly. "They've just come back from town."

They all fell silent as they waited for the two women to come inside. The door creaked open, and Belinda stepped into the kitchen, followed closely by Alison. Rodney immediately introduced them.

"Belinda, this is Fergus, the owner of this property, and his son, Mitch," Rodney said, nodding toward them. Then, turning to the other woman, he added, "Alison is Jason's girlfriend. Meet Fergus and Mitch. Did I miss anyone?"

Rodney looked around, as if double-checking, before gesturing to Belinda. "Grab a couple more chairs, Belinda, and join us. Do you girls want a beer?"

Both women hesitated, exchanging a surprised glance before shaking their heads in unison. "No, thank you," Belinda said softly, still somewhat taken aback by Rodney's casual tone.

As they moved chairs toward the large table, the women seemed a little shocked by the informal nature of the conversation. Fergus noticed their surprise but chose not to comment. Instead, he focused on the warmth of the room, the growing conversation, and the sense of uneasy camaraderie that was beginning to form.

Sensing the tension in the room, Fergus decided to take the lead and broke the silence. "I'll start," he said, his tone calm but firm. "I inherited the entire property a little while ago," he continued, but he didn't go into further detail. "I'm here today with Mitch just to do some exploring." He paused, choosing his next words carefully. "I wasn't aware that anyone was living here, and I'd like to understand the full circumstances of why you're here."

The room grew silent. The four of them exchanged uncertain glances, the atmosphere thick with unease. Finally, Rodney cleared his throat and began to explain.

"About four years ago, Belinda and I were traveling around Australia in an old motorhome," he said, his voice steady, though there was an undercurrent of nostalgia. "It was fitted to a Ford Transit, and we started our journey from Geelong in Victoria." He glanced at Belinda, who gave him a small nod of encouragement.

"We were both working as chefs at a restaurant, that's how we met. After a while, we decided that a life on the road was far better than working for the tight-arsed prick who owned the place," Rodney added with a touch of humour, though there was a hint of bitterness in his tone. "So, we made a plan to travel around Australia, and the first step was to find a vehicle. We looked at a lot of options, but most were out of our price range. Eventually, we settled on the Ford Transit, it was affordable once we sold our cars and pooled our money."

He paused for a moment, and Belinda picked up the story. "We didn't know what to expect. We were just looking for a new adventure, a fresh start away from everything. The journey was supposed to be a way to escape the grind and find something that felt more authentic, more real. But, after a while, we ended up here..."

Rodney finished, his expression now more serious. "We didn't plan to stay, but things didn't exactly go as planned. We were traveling up the coast when we found this place. It seemed like a good spot to park up and catch our breath, but as time passed, we just... stayed." He shrugged, clearly uncomfortable with the admission. "And here we are."

Fergus listened quietly, absorbing their story. It was clear that their arrival here wasn't part of any long-term plan, but rather a series of circumstances that had led them to settle in a place they hadn't intended to call home. Still, Fergus couldn't shake the nagging feeling that something was being left unsaid.

Their journey up the West Coast of Australia had been an unforgettable adventure, taking them all the way to Broome, where they spent over twelve months. They had worked, enjoyed the climate, and soaked in the relaxed atmosphere of the tropics. However, as they traveled further, they realised that their spending was outpacing their earnings. More often than not, they found themselves needing to save up enough money just to get to the next town.

After nearly three years of working and traveling, they ended up in Cooktown, but their Ford motorhome had suffered a blown engine, and with no money for repairs, their options became limited.

In Cooktown, they both found work at different venues and rented a modest place just outside of town. The old motorhome was sold to a local mechanic, and they caught a bus to Mareeba to buy a second-hand Hilux ute. They returned to Cooktown with the vehicle, hoping it would be their new lifeline for the road.

It was around this time that Belinda had struck up a friendship with George, an older man who worked as a kitchen hand with her. One day, George told her that he was planning to move back to Brisbane, but that she could take over his house if she wanted it. George explained that the house belonged to his uncle, and he had been looking after it for years. He offered the house to Belinda and Rodney rent-free, as long as they agreed to keep it maintained.

The house was a bit run-down, still in need of repairs, but it was liveable. Most importantly, it meant they could save the $350 per week they had been paying for rent, which was a relief. The idea of moving to a more permanent place seemed like the right step forward.

Jason, who had been working as a barman alongside Rodney, was also looking for a place to live with his girlfriend, Alison. Rodney suggested that Jason and Alison move in with them at Shiptons Flat. He proposed that they share the big, free house in exchange for helping maintain it, making it a win-win situation for everyone.

It wasn't the ideal living arrangement, but it offered stability and a chance to save money. The promise of a rent-free life, though challenging with the property's upkeep, gave all of them a sense of security. The decision felt like the right one at the time, even if it meant living in a place that, for all its rustic charm, came with its own set of challenges.

"So, here we are, and I must add, loving it," Rodney concluded with a grin as he moved towards the fridge for more drinks. "So, what happens now?" he added, passing another beer to Fergus.

"I have no idea," Fergus replied, accepting the drink. "I have no plans for anything at this stage. As I said earlier, we're just out exploring right now. But I can't see why anything should change for you guys at this stage. When I do move out here, I'd most likely build somewhere around here, so you guys are fine here for now."

Rodney took a sip of his beer and leaned back in his chair. "There's a much bigger and better place just over the hill, you know."

Fergus raised an eyebrow. "The council boundary plans show it as the homestead," he said. "But when I saw this place, I thought I must have read it wrong. So this isn't the homestead?"

Rodney shook his head. "No, I think the other place was the main homestead, and this was the manager's house," he explained. "The other place is, or I should say was, quite a mansion in comparison to this."

"And nobody's living there?" Fergus asked.

"No," Rodney confirmed. "There's no power out there. I think the lines all went down in a bushfire many years ago. Plus, it's really out of the way and hard to get to, as the road is so rough. It's a fair way from here along this track."

Fergus nodded thoughtfully, jotting down Rodney's contact details along with his Little Mulgrave phone number. He also gave him his mobile number, though it was mostly unreliable where he lived and next to useless out here at Shiptons Flat. The mobile phones at the time were a far cry from today's models, bulky, brick-sized devices with a battery life of only around three hours.

Taking Rodney up on his offer to show him the way out to the bigger house, Fergus, Mitchell, Rodney, and Jason piled into the Land Rover. The track started off well enough for the first couple of kilometres, but then it headed towards a deep gorge, becoming increasingly rough. Huge craters marred the track, forcing Fergus to stop the vehicle and engage the low-range four-wheel drive.

The track squeezed between two towering hills, creating a narrow passage with jagged rocks and boulders on either side. As they continued, a large boulder, dislodged from higher ground, had rolled down into the track and now lay in the middle of the path. There was just enough space to squeeze the Land Rover past it. Fergus carefully manoeuvred the vehicle, trying not to scrape the sides of the rugged terrain, while the others watched intently.

"Not exactly the smoothest of roads," Mitchell muttered, looking out the window at the imposing rock formations.

Fergus chuckled, keeping his focus on the track ahead. "Guess you could say it's got character."

Jason grinned. "Yeah, and we haven't even hit the worst of it yet."

The bumpy journey continued, with the Land Rover expertly handling the rough terrain, as they made their way towards the elusive "bigger house" that might hold some more information of the property's past.

Once past the gorge, the land opened up to rolling, lightly timbered hills, and the track began to climb away from the gorge. At this point, they reached a 'Y' intersection, where the track split into two directions, one to the left and the other straight ahead. As they continued forward, a herd of about thirty cattle scattered, startled by the noise of the car, and scrambled up a timbered incline, disappearing out of view.

"Who's cattle?" Fergus asked, intrigued.

"Probably yours," Rodney replied, "There are quite a few around, and I've never seen anyone come past the house to check on them. I've never seen them mustered either, but I'm sure there's no other way into this area except past the house. You need to veer to the right here; going left will take you over the mountain and down to the beach. There are some really nice beaches, but watch out for the crocodiles, there are plenty of them down there."

Fergus nodded thoughtfully, taking in the information as they steered the Land Rover to the right. The track ascended over a ridge, and the country flattened into an almost level expanse. It was lightly timbered with well-grassed fields, and in the distance, the Annan River could be seen winding its way through the landscape. It was becoming clear that this track might indeed be the only access to this area.

As the homestead finally came into view, Fergus couldn't help but be struck by its presence. From a distance, the house appeared majestic, sitting atop a rise with a commanding view that gave anyone approaching the impression of being announced before they even arrived.

"Well, you couldn't sneak up on it, could you?" Fergus remarked as he gazed at the impressive structure.

The house sat proudly on a batter that had been carved into the slope of the hill, giving it an air of dignity. Its white-painted walls gleamed in the sunlight, with a pale eucalyptus green corrugated iron roof that added to its refined look. However, as they drew closer, the true state of the house became evident. The grandeur of the home was marred by years of decay. The full-length verandah that wrapped around all four sides of the house had hardwood timber decking that had deteriorated in places, creating hazards for anyone attempting to walk to the front door. The door itself was locked, but Rodney knew exactly where the key was hidden, on top of the front door's toplight framing.

Fergus stood quietly for a moment, surveying the house. The stately appearance was undeniable, but it was clear that years of neglect had taken their toll. Despite its dilapidation, there was still something dignified about the place, as if it had once been a grand home but was now slowly being swallowed by time.

Rodney paused for a moment, as if collecting his thoughts, then continued as he slid the key into the lock and turned it. The heavy door creaked slightly as it opened, revealing the faded grandeur of the house's interior.

"An old bloke at the bowls club told me where this place was," Rodney said, his voice lowering slightly as he recalled the information. "We've been inside and had a look, but we didn't touch anything, as the old guy advised us not to. He said it's supposed to be a shrine of some sort, and that we'd be better off not disturbing anything. He promised he'd tell us the full story one day."

Rodney gestured toward the house, his eyes scanning the rooms beyond the threshold. He stepped aside, allowing Fergus and Mitchell to enter, before continuing, "Apparently, the old bloke used to be the manager here, and when this place was still operational, he lived over at your place, back at the flat."

Fergus raised an eyebrow at the mention of the "old bloke." He was curious but didn't press for more just yet, as he took in the sight of the house before him. The air felt thick with history, and there was a strange energy about the place, like it was holding on to long-forgotten secrets.

The hallway they stood in was wide and grand, though dust-covered and dimly lit. The smell of aged wood and stale air lingered in the space, and sunlight struggled to penetrate the gloom, filtering through thick curtains. The walls, once pristine, were now faded and peeling in places. Still, despite the wear and tear, there was an undeniable sense of past glory in the architecture, tall ceilings, intricate woodwork, and stone fireplaces that had clearly been designed to impress.

Rodney stepped inside, gesturing to the space. "It's hard to imagine what it used to be like, isn't it? The old guy said this place was once the hub of everything, a thriving homestead. But look at it now…" His voice trailed off as he walked into the main living room, where the furniture still sat as if frozen in time, though dusty and worn, it was clear this room had once been the centre of much activity.

Fergus followed, still eyeing the details around him. "A shrine?" he asked, his interest piqued. "What kind of shrine?"

Rodney shrugged as he looked around the room, clearly just as puzzled as Fergus. "That's what he said, mate. Never really elaborated on it. All he told me was that it's got something to do with the history of the place, maybe something to do with the old owner. But like I said, he said he'd tell us one day."

Jason, who had been standing by the door, added in a quiet tone, "There are a lot of rumours about this place. Some say it was more than just a house, that it had... meaning, like some kind of historical significance. But who knows? We were just told to keep our distance and not disturb anything. I guess it's not really our place to poke around too much."

Fergus nodded thoughtfully, his curiosity growing. "The manager... and this shrine idea... It sounds like there's a lot more to this house than just its looks." He turned toward Rodney, who seemed to be absorbed in his thoughts about the place. "If the manager lived here, what happened to him?"

Rodney glanced over at Fergus, his expression a mixture of puzzlement and hesitation. "I don't know all the details," he admitted. "But the old bloke seemed to think it was something... important. He said he couldn't say much more, but maybe one day he'd fill us in. It's all a bit of a mystery, really."

Fergus and Mitchell exchanged glances. The more they learned about this place, the more layers seemed to unfold, each more intriguing than the last. It was clear now that Stezland was more than just a piece of land, it was a place steeped in history, riddled with untold stories, and possibly, if they were lucky, secrets waiting to be uncovered.

As they walked through the front door into the entry vestibule, their footsteps echoed slightly on the spotted gum timber floor, its rich grains barely visible beneath a thick layer of dust. The house, though aged and forgotten, still bore traces of its former life. It was furnished, but everything, every surface, every piece of furniture, was coated with a fine layer of dust, as though time had suspended its passage in this house. A sense of stillness lingered, punctuated only by the soft creaks of the timber underfoot.

The air was thick with a musty, dank smell, the kind of stale scent that you might expect from a house that had been shut up for years. It clung to the fabric of the chairs, the curtains, and even the air itself, and seemed to press down on them, almost tangible. Fergus wrinkled his nose slightly, his eyes scanning the dim interior, taking in the details. It was clear this house had seen better days, but there was still a certain stately charm about it, though hidden under years of neglect.

A grand staircase led up to the second floor, its banister covered in dust, and the hallways stretched out to the left and right, each doorway leading to rooms that were still furnished, still holding onto their past identity. A large mirror hung on one wall, its surface tarnished but still reflecting faintly, adding to the sense of faded grandeur.

Mitchell's hand instinctively moved to his nose, trying to mask the overpowering scent, but his eyes, like his father's, were drawn to the remnants of a life once lived here. An old armchair sat in the corner of one room, a collection of tarnished silver frames resting on a console table, their contents long obscured by the years of dust. The curtains, once a vibrant colour, now hung limp, their fabric stiff from disuse.

Fergus stood for a moment in the doorway of the main living room, looking around. "It's like stepping into a different era," he murmured, more to himself than anyone else. The house seemed frozen in time, its secrets buried beneath the layers of dust and decay. It wasn't just an old building, it was a monument to a life and era long gone.

Rodney, who had followed them inside, spoke up softly, almost reverently. "There's a lot more to this place than just the house. The old guy, George, he told us there were some things here that shouldn't be touched. He said there were stories tied to everything, the furniture, the walls, even the dust."

Fergus gave Rodney a sidelong glance. "And what kind of stories are we talking about?"

Rodney shifted slightly, looking uncertain. "I don't know. Like I said, he wouldn't say much. But there's more to this place than meets the eye, that's for sure."

Mitchell, his curiosity piqued by the atmosphere and the mystery of the house, stepped further into the vestibule. His gaze wandered over the room, settling on an old grandfather clock in the corner, its hands frozen in time. "What happened to the people who lived here?" he asked, breaking the silence.

Rodney sighed, scratching the back of his neck. "I wish I knew, mate. It's all part of the mystery, I suppose. The old guy never said much about them. But something tells me they didn't just leave this place behind without a reason."

As Fergus and Mitchell exchanged a glance, the weight of Rodney's words sank in. The house was more than just an abandoned relic, it was a puzzle, a place full of unanswered questions. And somewhere deep within, it seemed to be waiting for them to uncover its secrets.

To the left of the entry, a doorway opened into a corridor, with another doorway to the left leading into the kitchen. The kitchen was spacious and well-equipped, featuring a large double-oven fuel stove range positioned halfway along the right-hand wall as you entered. In the centre of the room, a large square table took pride of place, surrounded by ample space, while two kitchen sinks were positioned against the left-hand wall.

At the far end of the room, another doorway led into a smaller dining or breakfast room, which offered a stunning view back down the valley they had just driven through through a large window.

Exiting the kitchen and returning to the corridor, an opening to the right led to a small area, roughly 1.6 meters by 1.2 meters, with doors on either side that led to powder rooms. The layout created a smooth flow from one space to another, combining both functionality and comfort.

Further along the corridor, the next door to the left opened into a spacious rectangular room, approximately five meters wide by eight meters deep. In the centre of the room stood a long dining table, flanked by five chairs on each side. To the left, an enormous fireplace stretched across one wall, adding warmth and grandeur to the space, while a large window at the front of the room allowed for an abundance of natural light to fill the space.

A doorway to the left of the dining area led into another room of similar proportions, where a full-size billiard table took centre stage. Around the billiard table, lounge chairs were arranged to face a large window on the opposite side of the room, offering a perfect view of the surrounding landscape. On the right-hand side of the room stood a bar, with a magnificent gun cabinet mounted behind it, adding a touch of elegance and a sense of history to the room.

The other side of the entry led to four bedrooms, each complete with a bed, furniture, and ensuites. The fifth bedroom, the largest of them all, also had an ensuite but was completely devoid of furniture. It was evident that the carpet had been pulled up from the floorboards, leaving the wooden surface exposed.

The rest of the house comprised a laundry, another bathroom, and a utility room situated behind the entrance vestibule, with a door leading outside to the rear of the house, where a two-bedroom, self-contained caretaker's unit was located.

The wood paneling and wallpaper were peeling from the walls, and the ceilings had begun to sag in some areas, adding to the house's neglected feel. Fergus noticed that the internal structure of the partition walls consisted of 150 series concrete masonry blocks, lined with 13mm plasterboard. This led him to believe that the external walls were likely made from 200 series concrete masonry blocks, with plasterboard on the interior and cement rendering on the exterior. Based on these materials, Fergus deduced that the house wasn't as old as it appeared at first glance, despite its weathered appearance.

There were several other buildings scattered around the property, each one clearly showing the ravages of time and neglect. The roofs were sagging, walls cracked, and some of the windows had long since shattered, leaving only dusty frames behind. Despite their curiosity, they decided not to investigate further; the day had already started to fade into evening, and the air was growing cooler.

With the light beginning to wane, they turned back toward the first house, Rodney's place, as Fergus had taken to calling it, since it was the only reference point they had. They had no better name for it, and it seemed fitting for the time being. As they retraced their steps, the tracks became a little more treacherous, with the fading light making it harder to navigate. But soon enough, they arrived back at Rodney's place, where the warmth of the house and the sense of familiarity offered a welcome reprieve from the long day of exploration. The houses they had seen earlier, with their peeling paint and deteriorating structures, felt like distant memories now as they returned to the safer, more lived-in environment of Rodney's home.

"That place is amazing,"Fergus said, his voice filled with excitement. "It's such a grand homestead, that's for sure. I'd love to know the story behind it, there's got to be one. The history here feels like it's waiting to be uncovered."

Jason, sensing Fergus's curiosity, offered, "Well, check out the bowling club. It's Saturday, so there's a good chance the old bloke will be there. He might have some answers for you."

Rodney added, chuckling, "His name's Colin. I remember now that the barman always called him 'Crazy Col'. If anyone knows the tale of that house, it's him. He's been around forever, always got some kind of story up his sleeve."

Fergus raised an eyebrow at the mention of "Crazy Col," intrigued by the nickname. 'Crazy Col, huh? That's a good start,' he said with a smile. 'Let's head over to the club then and see what we can learn.'

Rodney nodded and stood up. 'You might get more than you bargained for with Col, but it's worth a shot. He's lived here longer than anyone else, and the locals swear he knows everything about this place, even if he's a bit eccentric.'

They were back in Cooktown by around four o'clock, and Fergus decided to take a stroll to the Bowls Club while Mitchell stayed behind at the motel to rest and watch television.

To Fergus's surprise, there were no bowls games scheduled for that day, even though it was a long weekend. As he walked past the two well-maintained bowling greens toward the main entrance, he noticed a sign hanging on the fence that read, 'Whites Only on Weekends.' He couldn't help but chuckle. He knew exactly what it meant but found himself wondering how the club managed to get away with it in today's world.

The Cooktown Bowling Club was a familiar sight, just like nearly every other bowling club in country towns. It had floor-to-ceiling windows that overlooked the greens, giving a clear view of the play. The bar at the far end, directly facing the greens, was surrounded by stools, while tables and chairs filled the space between the bar and the windows. To the far right was the kitchen and dining area, and to the far left, tucked away from the main social area, was the pokie room. The place was filled with the usual crowd, familiar faces and regulars who seemed to all blend together in the same small-town community.

As Fergus approached the bar, he quickly spotted the man he was looking for. He was seated at the very end of the bar, where it curved to meet the wall, offering him an excellent vantage point to observe both the greens and anyone entering the club. The man had a nearly empty ten-ounce beer glass in front of him. In Queensland, this size was known as a "Pot," though in New South Wales it went by the name "Middy."

The barman had been watching Fergus as he walked toward the bar, anticipating that he'd order a drink. From the way Fergus was dressed and his posture, the barman quickly assumed he'd be after a "Schooner," the Queensland version of a fifteen-ounce beer. As Fergus reached the bar, the barman grabbed a schooner glass from the fridge, ready to serve him.

"Schooner?" asked the barman.

"Sounds good to me," Fergus replied, then, taking a chance, added, "And a Pot for Col too, thanks."

Colin, seated at the end of the bar, heard the stranger's comment and immediately his mind raced. Who the hell is this? he thought. It had been getting harder and harder to remember things, especially the names of people he hadn't seen in a while. But he was certain he didn't know this man, and he was also sure that this bloke wasn't from around here.

"My name is Fergus Laird," Fergus continued, "and I was hoping I might be able to have a chat with you."

"Well," Colin started, eyeing Fergus warily, "it depends on what it is that you're after. I'm pretty busy right now, as you can see," he added with a chuckle.

Fergus, undeterred, pressed on. "I was wondering if you know the name, Stephen Murray?"

Before he had even finished saying the name, Colin's face went ashen, and his eyes narrowed as he stared at Fergus, disbelief written all over his face.

"What if I do?" The jovial tone in Colin's voice had completely evaporated, replaced by a steely edge. "You'd do well to keep that prick's name out of your mouth around here."

Fergus hesitated for a moment before continuing. "He died a little while, "

"That's the news I've been waiting to hear for a long, long time," Colin interrupted, his voice suddenly filled with venom. "That prick should've died years ago." The old man looked almost gleeful. Then, his expression shifted, and he leaned forward, scrutinising Fergus. "But who the hell are you to come in here and tell me this? What's going on?"

Fergus didn't tell Colin that he had met Stephen Murray in prison. Instead, he offered a more ambiguous explanation. "I inherited some property through some business dealings from many years ago," he said, carefully choosing his words. "I want to find out more about it, and I heard you were once the manager there."

Colin studied him for a moment, his eyes assessing Fergus as if weighing his words. After a long pause, he sighed deeply, his voice growing more serious.

"For me, Fergus, this is a very painful story," Colin admitted. "It's one I haven't told in quite a while now, and maybe it's better off left buried. But you've given me great news today, the bastard's dead. And for that, I'll tell you the story. But I'll warn you, you may not have enough money to pay for all the beers it'll take to hear it."

Then, with a sly grin, Colin added, "Let's get away from these nosy bastards, though," nodding toward the barman who had been hovering nearby since Fergus had arrived.

Fergus smiled back, understanding the unspoken request, and the two men made their way to a table, ready to dive into a story that was long buried, but now, finally, ready to be told.

As they organised another round of drinks and settled down at a table by the window, Fergus couldn't shake the feeling that his old mate Stez might not have been all he seemed. Mentally, he steeled himself for the kind of information that might not be good news. Colin Freebody, it seemed, was about to unveil the full history of the property Fergus had casually named 'Stezland.' Fergus was beside himself with curiosity and apprehension.

"The old bloke was a good man," Colin began, his voice steady as he looked out over the bar. "He'd done a lot for me. Even when he only had that old original place, around three hundred acres, me and him were running cattle through the national park without anyone knowing the difference. More than a few times, we raised eyebrows at the cattle sales, selling such a large volume of store cattle in such good condition from such a small property."

Colin paused, taking a sip of his drink, then continued, his eyes narrowing as he began to speak of 'Old Ron Murray.'

"Ron Murray started his small cattle property at Shiptons Flat, but he wasn't just farming the land. He'd managed to help himself to using the crown lands around the area as his own personal cattle run," Colin said with a wry smile, recalling the old man's audacity. "Most of the land around the Cedar Bay mountain ranges had been set aside for tin mining back in the 1870s. But by the 1970s, the hippies moved into the abandoned tin mines, and the Bjelke-Petersen government sent in the police to clear them out, destroy their commune."

Colin's voice hardened as he continued. "That worked out great for Ron. He was blaming the hippies for the loss of some of his cattle, but he was way ahead of the government. He started tracking down the tin miners well before the police moved the hippies on. And he began buying up their mines, along with any freehold properties he could get his hands on."

Fergus leaned forward, now completely absorbed. Colin's voice lowered, as though he was sharing something deeply personal.

"See, Ron had a small acreage at Shiptons Flat, where he lived with his wife, Marge, and his son, David. Both he and his son started working for Ron Murray full-time, building cattle yards on various parts of Ron's growing property. Many of the leases Ron had secured also came with accommodation buildings, left behind by the miners. It was a strategic move, Ron recruited Aboriginal males from Wujil Wujil, trained them as stockmen, and let them live in those old miner cottages with their families in return for their work each year for mustering and other jobs around the property."

Colin's voice softened with the weight of the history he was revealing. "Ron didn't just offer them work; he provided them with as much fresh beef as they wanted, a way of keeping his cattle from being stolen. It was a system, a partnership in some ways, although there were always rumours about just how much 'business' was done behind the scenes."

Fergus was quiet for a moment, processing the complexity of the story unfolding before him. The landscape of his inherited property was beginning to reveal layers of history, of shadows and unsavoury deals. As Colin continued his tale, Fergus couldn't help but feel that there were still many secrets waiting to be uncovered.

Ron had lived alone in the 'Gatehouse,' the very same place where Rodney, the hippie, and his companions were now residing. Ron's estranged wife, on the other hand, lived with their son Stephen in the Cairns suburb of Manunda. Stephen would occasionally come out to Shiptons Flat during school holidays to help around the property, but each visit usually ended in arguments with his father. Every time, Stephen would leave, vowing never to return, only to come back again the following year, repeating the cycle.

Despite these tensions, life at Shiptons Flat seemed to be going well. Ron had begun breeding cattle better suited to the rugged, heavily timbered slopes around the Cedar Bay area by introducing Aberdeen Angus to this part of his property. To the west of the flat, he maintained a herd of Drought-master cattle, creating a diverse and resilient operation. With this, Ron managed to have the best of both worlds, and things only improved for him.

But in 1955, tragedy struck. Ron, at just fifty years old, suffered a heart attack. It was a shock to everyone who knew him, especially to Colin Freebody, who had worked alongside him for so long. Ron's estranged wife had the funeral held in Cairns, and his body was laid to rest in the Cairns Cemetery. Colin often wondered if she would have even bothered with the funeral at all, had she known that Ron had left his entire estate to their son Stephen, leaving her completely out of his will.

At the funeral, Stephen approached Colin and asked if he would stay on at the property to manage it for him. Colin, loyal as ever, agreed. Stephen promised that he would move into the 'Gatehouse' and work with Colin to ensure the property remained viable. But it seemed that Ron's death had also brought about a sudden shift in fortunes for his son.

Stephen, having carefully inspected the 'Gatehouse,' decided he wanted something more. He told Colin that he planned to build a new house some distance away from the 'Gatehouse,' on the rise where the grand homestead now stands. Stephen offered Colin the 'Gatehouse' as his new residence if he wished, a generous gesture given their complicated history.

For Colin, the timing was perfect. Things with his wife, Marge, were strained, and the 'Gatehouse' provided a peaceful retreat. It was a much more comfortable arrangement for him and his son, David, who was also working on the property. The 'Gatehouse' became a refuge for Colin, a place to escape from the tumult of his personal life and focus on the work that he knew so well.

Stephen had engaged a well-known architect from Cairns to design and supervise the construction of his new home, a project he had been eagerly anticipating for months. The plans were ambitious, and the house was expected to be completed in just under twelve months. Every day, like clockwork, trucks loaded with building materials drove past the 'Gatehouse,' their wheels kicking up dust as they made their way to the site where Stephen's grand vision was slowly beginning to take shape. The sound of machinery and the sight of construction workers became a constant presence in the area, signalling that this was no ordinary building project, it was a life-changing one for Stephen, marking the beginning of a new chapter in his life.

While the house was being built, Stephen was enjoying a holiday in the Philippines, a place he had always dreamed of visiting. It was here, amidst the vibrant streets and lush landscapes, that he met a 17-year-old Filipino woman who immediately caught his eye. She was beautiful, lively, and full of charm, and Stephen quickly found himself drawn to her. Before long, they were talking of marriage, and her parents, adhering to their cultural traditions, informed him of the dowry they required for the union, a monthly payment of the equivalent of two hundred and fifty Australian dollars. The dowry was based on what the young woman earned to support her family, a practice that Stephen initially understood, though the financial commitment weighed on him.

Calculating the long-term cost of the dowry, which would amount to around three thousand dollars a year, Stephen realised he needed to be absolutely certain that the woman he was about to marry was in good health. The prospect of such an ongoing financial commitment made him pause. He insisted she undergo a full medical examination to ensure there were no hidden issues that might complicate their future together. When the doctor's report came back, it contained unwelcome news: the young woman had a heart murmur, a condition that might require heart surgery in the near future to correct. This revelation was a blow to Stephen, who had already been weighing the financial implications of the dowry.

Faced with this unexpected obstacle, Stephen made the difficult decision to call off the wedding. While he regretted the turn of events, he felt it was the right choice, especially considering the potential medical risks. However, the girl's family, desperate to salvage the situation and keep the dowry arrangement intact, was beside themselves with worry. They offered a solution: her younger sister, just 16 years old, could take her place. Stephen was initially taken aback by the offer, but after some reflection and further discussions, he agreed to consider the proposal, on the condition that the younger sister also undergo a full medical check-up to ensure she was healthy.

Stephen found himself in a difficult position, torn between cultural expectations, financial considerations, and his own reservations. But he knew he could not make a decision without understanding the health implications fully. As the situation unfolded, Stephen's experience in the Philippines became increasingly complicated, and he was forced to navigate a complex web of family pressures, financial commitments, and his own moral compass. Ultimately, the decision to go ahead with the marriage would hinge on the results of the younger sister's medical examination, a decision that would have lasting consequences for Stephen, his future, and the path he was forging with his new life in Australia.

At twenty-five years old, Stephen Murray was a millionaire, a cattle property owner with more wealth and success than many could dream of achieving in a lifetime. But now, in addition to his newfound fortune, Stephen had a Filipino wife whom he just knew would draw envious glances and whispers from his friends in Cooktown and Cairns. The allure of a young, exotic wife, who hailed from a faraway place, was not something lost on the people who had known him before his wealth and change in lifestyle. Stephen was fully aware of the effect she would have, and while it bothered him somewhat, he also couldn't help but feel a sense of pride. The jealousy of others, in his mind, was just another sign that he had made it, his life was on a trajectory that few could match.

Stephen had recently bought a house in Cooktown, a modest yet comfortable residence, which he and his new wife planned to call home until their grand new house, located beyond the 'Gatehouse,' was finished. The house in Cooktown would serve as their temporary base, a place to settle into while the construction of their permanent residence took shape. As the project progressed, Stephen's anticipation grew, he couldn't wait to move into the home he had dreamed of for so long, a symbol of his success and the life he had built.

The 'Murrays' cattle property, however, had never been referred to by any name other than "The Murray Property." It was simply the family's land, and the land had always been tied to the Murray name. This lack of a name had always intrigued Colin Freebody, who had worked for Ron Murray for years. One aspect that had always puzzled Colin was the name of the building on the property known as the 'Gatehouse.' To him, it seemed oddly named, as it wasn't located at the start of the property, but rather nearer to its centre. For years, he had wondered about its significance.

It wasn't until Ron Murray had explained the story behind the 'Gatehouse' that Colin understood the reasoning. As it turned out, the 'Gatehouse' had once marked the very end of the Murray property, back when the property consisted only of the land that lay between the 'Gatehouse' and the town of Cooktown. Ron had bought up the surrounding mining properties and additional land, expanding the Murray holdings to encompass the entire Cedar Bay Ranges. The 'Gatehouse' was no longer at the end of the property, it had now become the gateway to the Cedar Bay part of the Murray property, the entryway to the wild and untamed part of the land where Ron's cattle roamed.

This transformation of the land mirrored the transformation in Stephen's life. From humble beginnings to a successful cattle owner, he was beginning to shape his own legacy, just as Ron had done before him. The purchase of the new house, the property, and the growing sense of success in his life were all part of a larger story, a story that had begun long before Stephen took the reins, but one that he was now at the heart of, with his new wife and future ahead of him.

Stephen Murray believed he had it all, money, land, and a young wife whom he regarded as the most beautiful woman in the world. She was indeed pretty, there was no denying that, but there was something about her appearance that troubled him, something that made her look out of place. To Stephen, she sometimes appeared as though she were a child playing dress-up in her mother's clothes, wearing makeup that felt foreign to her youth. Despite this, he had convinced himself that she was the woman for him, the woman who would stand by his side as he built his legacy.

However, as they walked through town or entered local hotels, Stephen couldn't help but feel the stares. He knew that people were talking about him, whispering behind his back. At first, he convinced himself it was just jealousy, people couldn't fathom how he, a young millionaire with so much success, could end up with someone like her. But over time, the whispers grew louder, and the laughter more evident.

The tipping point came one afternoon when Stephen was walking down the street with his wife. They passed a group of people, and he overheard a large Aboriginal woman shout out to another woman across the street, "Look, there's that Murray cunt with the slant-eyed slut." The words cut through him like a knife, and Stephen's blood boiled. The group of men around them erupted into laughter, mocking him, laughing at his wife in a way that felt like an insult to his very being.

That moment shattered Stephen's sense of pride. The laughter echoed in his mind, and it became unbearable. He had always thought that money and status would shield him from such ridicule, but it was clear that his wealth couldn't protect his dignity. From that day on, Stephen made a conscious effort not to be seen in public with his wife. He took pains to avoid the townsfolk, to steer clear of any social interactions where he might risk further humiliation.

But even as he withdrew from the public eye, the taunts continued. Every time he walked down the street, someone would shout out, "Hey Murray cunt, where's your slant-eyed slut?" accompanied by mocking laughter. The pain of the insults was a constant reminder that, in the eyes of some, no amount of wealth could elevate his status or protect his reputation.

e new house, nestled on the slopes of the Cedar Bay Range, was finally complete. After months of construction, the sprawling property was now home to Stephen and his young Filipino wife. The house, grand and modern, was filled with new furniture, much of it sourced from Brisbane. It was a symbol of their new life together, but for Stephen, something had shifted.

Originally, he had planned a grand housewarming party to celebrate the completion of the new home. He envisioned inviting all the important people from town, showing off his success, and basking in the admiration of his peers. However, after overhearing the hurtful comments and realising that people were talking about him behind his back, Stephen reconsidered. The thought of having his new wife endure more public ridicule was unbearable. So, instead of a lively celebration, he made the move-in a quiet and private affair, keeping the grand house to himself and his wife.

But life in the new house quickly became monotonous. The grandeur of the property, with its sweeping views and expansive space, no longer held the same allure. Stephen soon grew bored, restless, and began taking frequent trips away from the property. He would head to Cairns, Townsville, and even Brisbane, sometimes for just a few days, other times for weeks on end.

What Stephen did during these trips was anyone's guess. He spent his time away drinking, meeting with acquaintances, or indulging in some other escapism, but he never shared the details. The one thing he was certain of, however, was that his wife was left alone in the large, empty house. Day after day, she stayed in the solitude of the Cedar Bay Range, isolated from the rest of the world, as Stephen immersed himself in his own pursuits.

When Stephen did return to the property, his interactions with Colin were brief and businesslike. He would inquire about the cattle, ask how things were going with the property, and check in on the various tasks that Colin had taken over. But Colin quickly realised that Stephen had lost all interest in the land he had inherited, the cattle he had once cared for, and the legacy he had been handed. The conversations, though seemingly focused on business, felt hollow, as if Stephen's heart was no longer in it.

To Colin, it became increasingly clear that Stephen was disconnected from the very thing that had once been his pride and joy. The property, the cattle, the life he had built, it all seemed distant to him now. Stephen's discontent, masked behind a veneer of success, was growing ever more evident, and his actions spoke volumes.

Stephen had made his way into Cooktown on a Saturday for the races, a regular event that brought together locals and visitors alike. He hadn't returned to the property until quite late that night. Colin, who had been at home alone, recalled hearing a car pull up late in the evening, which he assumed was David returning. However, he also thought he heard another car several hours later, though he wasn't entirely sure. Both Colin and David had been in Cooktown that day, Colin had spent his time at the Bowls Club, while David had gone to the races.

Upon returning to the 'Gatehouse,' Colin found that David hadn't come home yet, which wasn't entirely unusual given the late nature of the races. He hadn't thought much of it and retired early for the night, assuming David might have stayed in town after the event. But when Colin woke up the next morning, David still wasn't home. At first, he dismissed it as nothing more than a late return from a night out, but as Sunday wore on and David didn't show up, a sense of unease began to creep in. By Monday morning, Colin's concern had grown, and he decided to drive into Cooktown to see if he could track down his son.

His first stop was the Shell service station, where David's friend worked as a mechanic. The young man confirmed that he had gone to the races with David on Saturday, but after the event, David had left before it had even finished. The mechanic hadn't seen David since then, and he didn't have any idea where he could have gone. This left Colin feeling even more unsettled.

Returning to the property, Colin tried to shake off his growing anxiety and resumed his usual work around the property, hoping David would eventually return. But by Wednesday, there was still no sign of him. That afternoon, Colin drove to Shiptons Flat to check in with his wife and ask if she had seen or heard from their son. He knew she would be worried, but he was unprepared for her reaction when he asked if she knew where David was.

As soon as he mentioned it, she became frantic, her fear escalating into a full-blown panic. She immediately called the police to report David as a missing person. Colin's heart sank as the reality of the situation hit him, something was wrong, and he wasn't sure what had happened to his son, but he feared the worst. With each passing hour, his worry deepened, and the sense of dread that had been slowly building inside him now had a name: something had happened to David, and it was no longer just a matter of him being late.

The following Monday morning, as Colin was preparing for his day, a police car pulled up at the 'Gatehouse.' Two officers stepped out, their faces stern and full of concern. They were looking for David, asking Colin if he had seen or heard anything about his whereabouts. It was unlike David to be gone this long without contacting anyone, Colin told them. They probed further, asking if Stephen was around. Colin felt a knot tighten in his stomach as he explained that he had no idea where Stephen might be. He had been off on one of his frequent trips, as usual, and Colin hadn't heard from him in days.

He offered directions to the mansion, down the track about eight kilometres, veering to the right, and mentioned that if Stephen wasn't there, his wife would probably be home and might have some idea of his whereabouts. Just as Colin was about to leave in his ute, the police car returned from the direction of Stephen's house. Flashing their headlights at Colin, they signalled that they needed to speak with him.

The constable rolled down his window and, with a grim expression, delivered shocking news: "We're going to have to seal this gate down to Stephen's house and not let anyone through. There are two bodies down there. Most likely a murder-suicide."

Colin's heart stopped. "What? ... Stephen? ... and..." he stammered, his voice faltering as the weight of the situation hit him.

"Yes," the constable replied. "We don't know too much yet, but the evidence suggests that's what we're dealing with. I've left John down there while I head back to Cooktown to get more help from Cairns. I'll be back, hopefully before dark. Don't let anyone through, it's a crime scene."

The world seemed to shift beneath Colin's feet. He felt an intense wave of nausea wash over him, his hands shaking uncontrollably. As much as the news unsettled him, part of him wasn't completely shocked. Stephen had been acting strange for quite a while now, frequent, unexplained trips, his distant attitude, and the isolation he had placed his young wife in. She had been left alone in the big house while he wandered the country, drinking and living a reckless life. Colin had always been concerned for the young Filipino woman who had married Stephen, but now the gravity of the situation was sinking in.

"Oh, I wish David was here, he's missing out on all the excitement," Colin muttered to himself, though the words didn't bring him comfort.

The hours that followed were a blur. Vehicles came and went past the 'Gatehouse,' and as much as Colin tried to gather more information, nobody offered any further details. His mind raced, but the silence from the police and the locals left him feeling increasingly isolated.

It wasn't until around ten o'clock the next morning that another vehicle approached the 'Gatehouse', a flatbed truck with loading ramps. The driver stepped out and asked Colin for directions to the police crime centre. Confused, Colin explained how to get to the mansion, which, by now, he assumed had become the focal point of the investigation.

But nothing could have prepared Colin for what happened next. The truck returned an hour later, and with it came a heart-wrenching sight: David's ute, loaded onto the back of the flatbed truck.

Colin's legs buckled beneath him as a violent shock coursed through his body. He collapsed to the ground, gasping for breath. The police car trailing the truck had witnessed Colin's fall and immediately pulled over to assist. One of the officers quickly called for an ambulance from Cooktown.

As Colin lay there, trying to process the overwhelming wave of grief and disbelief, his thoughts tumbled like a cascade of chaos. David, his son, his flesh and blood, hadn't just gone missing. He was now part of this tragic and twisted nightmare. The impact of it all was too much to bear.

Colin slowly regained consciousness the following Wednesday at the Cairns Hospital, his mind foggy and disoriented. He had been airlifted from Cooktown by helicopter the previous day after collapsing in shock. The events that had unfolded over the past days seemed like a surreal nightmare. He tried to gather his thoughts, but his mind felt scattered. Why am I here? he wondered. What stroke? How could I have had a stroke? It didn't make sense. He tried to sit up, but his body was uncooperative. Then, as memories flooded back, the reality of the situation hit him with brutal force.

David. His son. David's ute. The flatbed truck. Why was David's ute there? He remembered the image of the truck hauling it, the sickening realisation that his son was somehow tangled up in this mess, in the same tragedy that had claimed Stephen's life. Stephen is dead. Why is David there? The questions seemed endless, and his mind couldn't latch onto a single answer. His head throbbed as if it were trying to process more than it could handle.

His eyes wandered to the call button on the bedside table. He tried to reach for it, but his right hand wouldn't move. Panic set in. He struggled again, trying to command his hand to move, but it remained still, unresponsive. With frustration mounting, he used his left hand to finally push the button. The buzzer emitted a soft, sharp beep. Within seconds, a nurse appeared, her calm demeanour a stark contrast to the storm raging inside him.

"Help," Colin whispered, his voice cracking as tears began to well in his eyes. The nurse quickly assessed him, offering comfort as she administered care. She explained that he had been given a strong sedative, and he had slept soundly until the early hours of the morning.

"You've had a stroke, Mr. Freebody," the nurse said gently. "But you're starting to recover. It will take time. The doctor will be in soon to explain everything, and the police are waiting outside to speak with you. Your wife will be here later this afternoon."

Colin's head spun. A stroke. He had no memory of it happening, no recollection of collapsing, or how he ended up in the hospital. His thoughts immediately returned to David. What about David? His son had been missing for days now, and the sight of his ute being hauled away in that truck was still fresh in his mind. His stomach turned again at the thought of him. Where is David?

When the doctor arrived, Colin was barely able to concentrate. The words were muffled, as if coming from a distance. The doctor explained that Colin had suffered a stroke, one that would leave him with lingering effects. He would recover some functionality but not completely, and the road ahead would be long and difficult. But Colin hardly heard the doctor's words. His mind was still trapped in the question that wouldn't go away: What happened to David?

Unable to hold back his frustration, Colin interrupted the doctor's explanation. "I need to know about my son. What's happening with David? Where is he?"

The doctor hesitated before responding, clearly uncomfortable with the question. "I'm afraid I don't know anything about your son, Mr. Freebody. I've only been briefed on your medical condition. The police are waiting outside to speak with you, and I'm sure they'll have more answers for you. I'll send them in shortly."

Colin's heart sank. The police. His pulse quickened. He wasn't ready to face them, wasn't ready to process whatever they might reveal. But he knew, deep down, that the answers wouldn't wait. The questions he had about his son, about Stephen's death, and about what had happened to the property and his family, it was all too much. He had to know, even if it tore him apart.

As the doctor left the room, Colin sat in silence, bracing himself for the conversation with the police. Every minute felt like an eternity. His mind raced with worry and fear for David, but as he sat there, waiting, he couldn't shake the feeling that the answers he was about to hear would change everything.

Sergeant John Collins, the lead detective from Cairns, entered Colin's hospital room with a quiet step, fully aware of the gravity of the situation. He approached Colin's bedside and gently introduced himself, but before he could say much more, Colin's voice cut through the silence, shaky but urgent.

"How's David? My boy, David... Is he in trouble? Did he kill Stephen?"

The detective froze, taken aback by the flood of emotions in Colin's words. He wasn't prepared for this kind of directness, and for a moment, he struggled to grasp the full scope of the situation. His mind raced, but he didn't know how to respond to Colin's question.

"Er, Mr. Freebody," Sergeant Collins stammered, trying to collect his thoughts. "I think you may be a bit confused."

"But is David OK?" Colin repeated, his voice more insistent, tinged with worry. His desperation was palpable, his brow furrowed as he searched the detective's face for answers.

The detective paused, taking a deep breath, and spoke slowly, his words heavy with sorrow. "David is deceased, I'm afraid," he said softly, making sure every word was clear and unmistakable. "His body was identified by your wife, from photographs of his tattoos on the back of his calves."

Colin's heart seemed to stop. The room spun, and he could hardly process what he was hearing. His eyes glazed over, and he stared blankly at the wall behind the detective, as if he were trying to escape the harsh reality of the words. The detective continued asking Colin a few more questions, but there was no response. Colin was lost in shock, his mind unable to comprehend the words or the gravity of the situation. His world had just shattered, and he was too overwhelmed to react.

After a few moments, the detective realised that Colin was in no condition to answer any more questions. He called for the nurse, who immediately arrived to assist. The detective, recognising that there was nothing more to be done for the moment, quietly left the room.

Later that afternoon, Marge, Colin's wife, arrived at the hospital. Her face was tear-streaked, and her eyes were swollen from hours of crying. The moment she laid eyes on Colin, both of them broke down in uncontrollable sobs, the weight of the news crashing over them. Marge sank into the chair beside Colin's bed, trying to gather herself enough to speak, but the emotions were overwhelming.

Finally, after several minutes of silence, Marge began to speak through her tears. "It was just horrible," she whispered, her voice raw with grief. "They wouldn't let me see David's body. They only showed me two photographs of his tattoos. They wouldn't tell me why I couldn't see him. They just said it was better that I didn't."

She choked on her words, trying to steady her breath. "They told me that David's body, along with another person's, was found at the house on the property, but they wouldn't say anything more than that. They asked if the person in the photos was David, and I told them it was. I knew those tattoos. One of them had your name and mine in a scroll on his left calf. I knew it was him... But other than that, I don't know anything else. And now, I'm just... I'm just lost."

She broke down into tears again, clutching Colin's hand as if holding on to whatever was left of their family. Colin, still struggling to grasp the reality of the situation, felt his heart shatter again, the pain of losing David now compounded by the confusion and the fear of not knowing the full truth.

The room was filled with an unbearable silence, both of them lost in their grief, unable to comprehend the horrors that had unfolded in their lives.

When the two constables from Cooktown arrived at Stephen's house on Monday morning, the first thing that caught their attention was the Toyota Hilux utility parked in front of the house. It was an odd sight, considering they had been told to look for any signs of Stephen's whereabouts, but David's vehicle wasn't something they had expected to see. They approached the house and knocked on both the front and back doors several times, but there was no answer.

Growing more concerned, they decided to investigate further. The Hilux was unlocked, and upon checking the glovebox, they found the logbook. Their suspicions were confirmed: the vehicle belonged to David Freebody, a key figure in the case they had been investigating.

One constable stayed by the vehicle, while the other began circling the house, inspecting the verandah and trying to peer inside the windows. All of them were covered with netting curtains, obscuring any view. It was then that the constable heard a faint buzzing sound. He turned and noticed an alarming sight, an overwhelming number of blowflies between the glass window and the curtain netting. Something was terribly wrong.

He immediately called for his partner, who quickly joined him. The two officers made a hasty decision to break a window panel in the front door to gain entry. As soon as the door opened, a putrid stench overwhelmed them, and one constable staggered back outside, gasping for air, struggling to suppress the bile rising in his throat.

The other constable, determined to find the source of the foul odour, braved the interior of the house. The stench led him to the main bedroom, where the gruesome discovery awaited. Two bodies, covered in flies and maggots, lay lifeless on the king-size bed, surrounded by a pool of dried blood. The sight was so horrific that the constable barely made it past the doorway before he turned and fled, unable to contain his nausea.

The shock of the scene left both officers momentarily frozen. After a few moments to regain their composure, they realised the severity of the situation. One constable remained at the scene, securing the area, while the other rushed back to the Cooktown police station to call for backup and additional assistance. The horror they had stumbled upon was far beyond what either of them had anticipated, and they knew the investigation was about to take a dark and tragic turn.

At 11 AM on Monday morning, Sergeant John Collins and Detective Chris Murphy were dispatched from Cairns Police Headquarters to investigate the scene. They arrived at the Cooktown Police Station by 3 PM, where they were met by two members of the forensic science team from Mareeba Police Station, who had been briefed by the constable who had made the initial discovery. Together, they gathered their equipment and set off for what had become known as "the house on the Murray property."

By the time they arrived at the property around 7 PM, the detectives were faced with a scene that was even more harrowing than they had anticipated. Though no official identification had been made, it was clear that the female body found on the king-size bed was highly likely to be that of Stephen Murray's wife, as indicated by various photographs from around the house. The grim task of identifying the male body proved far more challenging. The face of the body, presumed to be that of Stephen Murray, had been badly disfigured by what appeared to be a shotgun blast, making it nearly impossible to confirm his identity through visual means alone.

Despite the difficulty in confirming the identity of the male body, the evidence pointed strongly in that direction. The vehicle parked outside the house, which had been identified as belonging to David Freebody, added another layer of complexity to the case. David was now considered a person of interest, and the detectives couldn't ignore the possibility that he might hold crucial information regarding the events that led up to this horrific scene.

The forensic team went to work, carefully documenting the scene and collecting evidence, while the detectives began to formulate their next steps. The investigation was far from straightforward, and with so many unanswered questions, Collins and Murphy knew they were just beginning to unravel the tangled web of tragedy that had unfolded on the Murray property.

The bodies were carefully transported to Cairns that night, where they were to be processed and prepared for identification. The following morning, efforts were made to find people who could provide any information that might lead to a positive identification of the bodies. Given the severe disfigurement of the male body, particularly the face, it was decided that a more reliable method of identification would be to focus on other distinguishing features. The detectives turned to the tattoos on the back of the male's calves, which were known to be distinctive, as they had been previously photographed.

Stephen Murray's mother was contacted and shown these photographs, in the hope that she could help confirm the identity of the deceased. She was asked to examine the images of the tattoos on her son's left calf. As she studied the photographs, her face grew increasingly tense, and after a long moment, she firmly stated that the body was not her son's.

Her reaction was unequivocal. She stated that she was absolutely certain that the body before her was not Stephen's, despite the presence of the tattoos. This revelation left the detectives in a state of confusion. The tattoos had been so distinctive, so deeply personal, that it seemed unlikely anyone else could have had the same markings. But the mother's words were clear. If the body wasn't Stephen's, then who was it? And where was Stephen Murray?

The detectives, now faced with more questions than answers, realised they would need to dig deeper into the investigation. The absence of a clear identification from the mother only added to the mystery surrounding the two bodies found at the Murray property.

Colin Freebody was in no condition to assist with the identification of the bodies. His physical and emotional state left him unable to process the harrowing reality of what had unfolded. Meanwhile, his wife, Marge, was found in the waiting room of the Cairns hospital, still in shock and grief-stricken. She was shown the photographs of the bodies, and after a brief pause, she confirmed with certainty that the body in question was indeed that of their son, David.

The police, piecing together the sequence of events, hypothesised that Stephen Murray had returned from the races in Cooktown on Saturday night to find David Freebody in his home, presumably in his bed with his wife. This was where the bodies were discovered, leading the investigators to believe the murders occurred in the bedroom. The scenario was assumed to unfold with Stephen discovering the two of them together, enraged by the situation. In a fit of fury, it was believed that Stephen had retrieved a 12-gauge shotgun from the gun cabinet in the billiard room and returned to the bedroom, where he shot both victims. Despite a thorough search of the crime scene, no spent shotgun shells or the weapon itself were found.

However, an autopsy report revealed vital evidence that supported the theory. The report confirmed the presence of 9mm shot, composed of pure lead and antimony, which was consistent with 12-gauge shotgun cartridges known as "Triple A's," containing 9 x 9mm balls. David Freebody had been shot in the face, and Stephen's wife had been shot in the back of the head.

The bodies had not been discovered until eight days after the killings, which meant the rapid decomposition had set in due to the extreme heat. The situation was becoming more dire, and the police were now actively searching for Stephen Murray.

Colin paused before continuing. "And," he added, "the police had searched the house and removed the firearms and ammunition from the gun cabinet in the billiard room. They sealed the house, locking it up with police seals."

Colin's voice grew heavier as he spoke of the aftermath. "The house remained locked until Stephen was eventually captured in a small town in Victoria. He was sent back to Brisbane for trial. Shortly after that, his attorney came to the house with removalists, and much of Murray's belongings were taken away. The bed where the bodies were found, the mattress, the carpet from the bedroom, everything was hauled off. They set it all on fire beside the house."

Fergus, who had been listening intently, went to the bar to refresh their drinks before returning to the table. "So, what happened to the house after that?" he asked, his curiosity piqued.

Colin sighed deeply. "Nothing. No one had been there since, except for the kids at the 'Gatehouse' and now you, as you've told me. The place just started to rot away slowly. I'll admit, I was tempted to burn it down, but I knew that would only land me in jail. It wasn't worth it. I left the 'Gatehouse' and went back with Marge. We needed each other after losing David. We were both grieving."

Fergus nodded solemnly, taking in the weight of Colin's words. After a pause, he stood up. It was half-past seven as he left the bowling club, making his way toward the RSL club's restaurant to grab a couple of takeaway pizzas. He walked back to the motel, passing by the traditional owners of the land who were calling out for cigarettes, beer, and money. "Fucking cretins," he muttered to himself as he moved on, their voices blending with the dusk. The weight of the story lingered in the air as Fergus made his way back, his mind swirling with the darkness of what had transpired at the Murray property.

Mitchell and Fergus decided to return to the "Murray house" the next morning, determined to do a more thorough exploration of the home. Their plan was to assess the possibility of bringing the property back to a liveable condition and potentially turning it into their new residence.

The second look at the house was somewhat disheartening for Fergus. As they stepped inside, he couldn't help but notice the extent of the deterioration that had become more apparent upon closer inspection. Time had taken its toll, and the house had been left to decay, seemingly untouched for years. There was a layer of dust on nearly everything, and the smell of neglect lingered in the air. Despite this, Fergus didn't feel deterred; rather, the challenge of restoring the house seemed more daunting, yet oddly appealing.

Fergus briefly glanced at the room where the tragic events had unfolded, the room where the murders had occurred. He expected it to be unsettling, but to his surprise, it didn't faze him as much as he had anticipated. The reality of it seemed distant, almost surreal. The room, with its dark memories, would likely be turned into his own personal bedroom. He found the idea of reclaiming the space strangely empowering, as if he could breathe new life into it, despite its grim history.

Mitchell, on the other hand, was more focused on the billiard room. He had already claimed the large, ornate billiard table for himself and was now on a mission to track down all the missing billiard balls and pool cues. It seemed trivial in comparison to the more pressing issues, but Mitchell found himself immersed in the task, perhaps as a way of distracting himself from the bigger picture.

Fergus, who had a more practical mindset, was thinking about the financial side of the project. The cost of restoring the house to its former glory would likely be extensive. He could already imagine the price of repairs, from fixing the crumbling infrastructure to replacing broken fixtures and updating outdated systems. However, he reasoned that, considering he had essentially acquired the house for nothing, the investment might still be worthwhile. It would probably cost as much to restore as it would to build a brand-new home, but the appeal of owning the historic property, with its rich past and potential, made it a risk worth taking.

As the two of them wandered through the dilapidated rooms, Fergus couldn't help but think about how the house could be transformed. He was aware of the work ahead, both physically and financially, but the challenge invigorated him. It was going to be a monumental task, but with Mitchell's enthusiasm for the billiard room and Fergus's determination to revive the entire house, they both felt a sense of purpose. They were ready to take on the monumental challenge of bringing the "Murray house" back to life.

That afternoon, as Fergus and Mitchell were leaving Shiptons Flat, they turned onto the quiet Mulligan Highway, their minds preoccupied with the day ahead. The sound of tires humming against the asphalt was broken by the sight of a police officer up ahead, standing by the side of the road and flagging them down. Fergus sighed, slowing down and pulling over behind the police Landcruiser. He rolled down his window as the officer approached their vehicle.

"Good afternoon, sir," the officer greeted. "I'm Senior Constable Kirkland, Queensland Police. I'm conducting random breath testing and require you to submit a sample of your breath."

Fergus nodded, his nerves steady. "Good afternoon," he responded.

"This is a breath-testing device," Constable Kirkland explained, holding it up for Fergus to see. "To comply with my requirement, I direct you to place your mouth over the mouthpiece of the device and blow directly and continuously until told to stop."

Fergus, accustomed to these kinds of checks, leaned forward and followed the officer's instructions. He had no reason to be concerned. He hadn't consumed alcohol since Saturday night, and after a good night's sleep and several meals, he felt completely sober.

"Commence blowing now… keep going… keep going… stop!" the officer instructed.

Fergus exhaled steadily, knowing the result would be negative. His mind was already shifting back to thoughts of the house and their plans for the next day. However, when Constable Kirkland examined the breathalyser's reading, the officer's demeanour changed slightly. There was a moment of hesitation, and he looked up from the device.

"You're borderline," the officer said, an edge of concern in his voice. "What have you been drinking?"

Fergus raised an eyebrow, irritated by the suggestion. "I haven't had a drink in days. I told you that," he replied, his patience beginning to wear thin.

The officer looked uncertain for a moment, then made a decision. "I'll have to arrest you for the purpose of conducting a breath analysis at the station. Please step out of the vehicle."

Fergus' reaction was swift and sharp. "Fucking bullshit! Grow up. What about my son? Are you taking him to

Cooktown too? You can't leave him here on his own. He's a minor, and I'm not leaving my vehicle here by the side of the road for very obvious reasons."

The officer hesitated, clearly thrown off by Fergus's quick response. "I… I thought he was an adult," he stammered, now unsure of himself, especially given that Fergus didn't seem intimidated like most motorists in such situations.

Fergus narrowed his eyes. "Well, he's a child. So I suggest you call for backup." He leaned back in his seat, his expression steely. "Then we'll get this sorted."

The officer, now realising his earlier lapse in judgment, straightened up, trying to regain control. "I'll decide when and if I call for backup," he said, his tone more authoritative. "In the meantime, I'll do a roadworthy check on your vehicle."

Fergus scoffed, his irritation mounting. "It's a new car, less than two thousand kilometres on it. There's nothing wrong with it."

At this point, his patience was running thin. His father had always had a notoriously short temper, and it seemed to run in the family, as Mitchell had demonstrated a similar streak when agitated. Fergus was trying to hold himself together, but the situation was beginning to push him over the edge. The officer was doing nothing to calm the tension, and it was clear that a simple breath test had escalated into something far more frustrating.

Fergus forced himself to take a deep breath, hoping that the situation would resolve itself without further conflict, but it seemed that Senior Constable Kirkland was determined to assert his authority, no matter how unnecessary the actions seemed.

As the police officer began walking around the car, Fergus glanced over at Mitchell, noticing the tight, tense expression on his face. He grinned, hoping to lighten the mood, but Mitchell's eyes were fixed forward, his face as grim as ever.

"What's wrong, Mitch?" Fergus asked, trying to break the uncomfortable silence.

Before Mitchell could respond, the unmistakable sound of glass shattering echoed from the back of the Landrover. Fergus turned to see the officer quickly striding back toward the driver's side window, an angry expression now replacing the earlier formality.

"You've got a broken tail light," the officer said, his voice stern. "I'm giving you a vehicle defect notice for that, and I'm also booking you for exceeding the speed limit by fifteen kilometres per hour. Hand me your license."

Fergus fought to maintain his composure, his knuckles turning white as he gripped the steering wheel. His lower lip was clenched tightly between his teeth, hard enough to make it bleed slightly, but he didn't care. His hands shook as he passed his license over to the officer.

Without missing a beat, the constable took the license and scribbled something down, then handed over the ticket. But when it came time to sign, Fergus simply shook his head, refusing to cooperate. The officer didn't even seem to care. He ripped the booking page off the clipboard and tossed it into the passenger seat with a deliberate flick of his wrist.

Sensing the growing frustration in Fergus, the officer swiftly returned to his police cruiser. The engine roared to life, and in moments, he was gone, driving off down the highway. Fergus, his jaw clenched and his muscles tight, remained still in his seat for a few moments. He let out a long breath, trying to regain his composure.

Finally, he turned to Mitchell, his voice quieter this time. "What's going on with you, Mitch? You've been off all day."

Mitchell didn't meet his gaze, his eyes still locked on the road ahead. After a long, tense pause, he spoke, his voice barely a whisper.

"That's the same cop that killed Mum."

Fergus's heart sank. The words hit him like a freight train, and he was left speechless, the weight of Mitchell's statement hanging heavily in the air between them. The entire situation, the breath test, the fines, the anger, suddenly felt insignificant in comparison to the dark, painful truth that Mitchell had just revealed. Fergus sat there in silence, unable to fully process what he had just heard, as the world around them seemed to close in with the echoes of a tragedy far too close to home.

Senior Constable Stanley Kirkland sat in his office at the Cooktown Police Station, his mind racing with the nagging feeling that something wasn't right. The name "Laird" had stuck in his mind like a splinter, refusing to leave. It wasn't a typical name, something about it seemed strangely familiar. And then, it hit him. Amelia Laird. The woman in the car whom he had pulled over near Cairns about five years ago. The memory of that day flooded back, vivid and jarring.

Kirkland remembered it as if it had happened just yesterday. He had been finishing up a routine traffic stop for speeding, his attention focused on issuing the fine, when he decided to pull back onto the highway. He hadn't looked in his rearview mirror. He hadn't even thought to. But Amelia Laird had been behind him, and somehow, she had seen him. Without warning, she swerved sharply to avoid him, her car spinning out of control and crashing head-on into a tree on the opposite side of the road.

What Kirkland would never forget, though, was the image of the young boy in the passenger seat, staring back at him through the side window as the car sped past. The crash had been violent, and Amelia Laird was killed instantly. The boy survived, barely, and in the aftermath, he became the key witness in the investigation. The child had claimed that Kirkland's police car had caused his mother to swerve, pointing out that he had seen the officer pull out in front of them, forcing her into the tree.

Kirkland, of course, had a different story. He testified that both cars had been well off the road when the woman suddenly swerved onto the wrong side and crashed. His testimony was accepted without question, while the child's account was dismissed as the ramblings of a traumatised boy.

Despite being cleared of all involvement, something about the incident had gnawed at Kirkland, especially since the boy's story had been so vivid, so clear. He had been fortunate that his superiors never pushed too hard, never dug too deeply into his actions that day. The missing notebook, along with the identity of the driver he had pulled over, was never found, and it had never been pursued. He had gotten away with it, or so he thought.

Now, here was the name "Laird" again, and it made his stomach tighten. Was it possible that the man he had pulled over earlier today was somehow connected to Amelia? A relative, perhaps? It seemed unlikely, but Kirkland couldn't shake the feeling that there was more to it than just coincidence. Even if there was a connection, so what? What did it matter now? He had been cleared. The case was closed.

But as an afterthought, his gaze drifted to the stack of paperwork on his desk. The infringement notices he had issued to Fergus, the man from earlier that day, were sitting there, ready to be processed. Without much thought, Kirkland grabbed the papers and tore them up, disposing of them without a second glance. He didn't want to deal with any fallout, didn't want to deal with any more complications. If Fergus ever made a fuss, if he raised a stink about the fines, it would open up old wounds, wounds Kirkland had carefully buried.

Despite his initial confidence in being cleared of wrongdoing five years ago, the fear of the past still lingered at the edges of his mind. The last thing he needed was for his superiors to start questioning him again, digging into his history, finding the missing details that could unravel the neat little story he had told about that tragic accident. He had been lucky once; he didn't want to test his luck again.

Stezland

Fergus and Mitchell finally arrived back at Little Mulgrave after their trip to Shiptons Flat. The landscape was familiar, the winding roads leading them back to their quiet, rural life. Mitchell had quickly fallen back into the routine of boarding school, as they had planned. It was an arrangement that allowed Fergus to focus on the ambitious task of refurbishing the house at Shiptons Flat.

The property, now officially known as Stezland, was a legacy that Fergus had inherited from his late friend in prison Stephen Murray. It was a significant change in their lives, and it was a shift that had started to influence Mitchell's own future. Originally, Mitchell had set his sights on pursuing a career in Medicine after finishing school, but now, with the prospect of managing the property and working with cattle, his ambitions were slowly changing.

The idea of Veterinary Science had begun to appeal to him. He had always been fascinated by animals, and the notion of combining his interest in biology with the responsibility of looking after livestock seemed like the perfect fit. His decision wasn't set in stone yet, but the thought of becoming a veterinarian felt more aligned with his future at Stezland.

Still, Mitchell had time. He wasn't due to graduate for another two years, and as planned, he would take a gap year afterward to explore his options, gain more experience, and perhaps work on the property during that time. That break could give him the clarity he needed to solidify his decision, and perhaps even help Fergus with the massive undertaking of setting up the property for cattle grazing.

For now, though, Mitchell was back at school, focused on his studies while the plans for Stezland slowly took shape. And Fergus, in the meantime, was immersed in the work of restoring the old house and getting everything ready for when they would finally make it their home. Their lives had taken a new direction, and both father and son were eager to make the most of the opportunity they had been given.

Fergus couldn't shake the uneasy feeling that lingered after his encounter with Senior Constable Stanley Kirkland near Cooktown. The exchange had been tense, and there was something about the officer's demeanour that rubbed Fergus the wrong way. Mitchell's comment about Kirkland's involvement in Amelia's accident made the situation even more unsettling. If what Mitchell said was true, and this was the same cop who had been a witness to that tragic crash years ago, Fergus couldn't help but wonder if things were about to get awkward, maybe even worse.

With the constable's name clearly printed on the infringement notice, Fergus decided to take action. He called his solicitor, Brian Haptu, who had been involved with the aftermath of Amelia's accident. After reviewing his files, Brian confirmed what Fergus had suspected: Senior Constable Stanley Kirkland was indeed the police officer who had witnessed the accident. The revelation struck Fergus like a punch to the gut. This wasn't just any random officer, this was the very same one whose testimony had been pivotal in the case. The same officer whose involvement had made the situation so murky in the first place.

Now, Fergus' concern wasn't just about the officer's role in the past incident. He began to think that Kirkland's presence in his life could become more than just a minor nuisance. The interaction on the road had been frustrating enough, but if Kirkland decided to pursue any further trouble, it could lead to more complications. He wasn't about to let someone like that cause unnecessary problems for him.

Fergus' mind started to drift to his days in Vietnam, where survival was the only rule that mattered. In the jungle, when a hazard presented itself, there was no room for hesitation. One didn't go around the danger, they eliminated it. With the clear and unflinching logic that had helped him survive in a war zone, Fergus began to consider how he might deal with Kirkland. Perhaps, he thought, it was time to remove the obstacle before it had a chance to grow into a real threat.

The thought lingered in his mind, unsettling yet oddly satisfying. If Kirkland continued to pose a problem, Fergus was prepared to take steps to ensure that his peace would not be disturbed. After all, he had learned long ago that some hazards didn't just go away on their own, they had to be dealt with head-on. But for now, he pushed the thought aside. It was a temptation, yes, but one he would resist… for the time being.

Fergus had reconnected with an old army buddy, Geoff Fawkner, who had transitioned into a career as a Building Surveyor for the Cairns Council. When Fergus reached out to see if Geoff would be interested in a trip to Cooktown to inspect a property for refurbishment, Geoff was immediately excited by the prospect.

"I'll pay you for your time, of course," Fergus had offered. "It's too rough to camp out there right now, so I'll cover accommodation, meals, and, of course, drinks at the pub in Cooktown."

Geoff, ever the easy-going mate, waved off the offer. "Mate, I should be paying you for such a holiday! Just let me know when, and I'm ready. Don't even think about offering me money again."

Fergus chuckled, "How about next Friday afternoon? I can pick you up from work if that suits."

Geoff thought for a moment and then replied, "How about pick me up from home on Friday morning? I'm not working that day, and June is going to Innisfail for the weekend with her mum."

The following Friday, they set off early from Cairns and arrived in Cooktown just after midday. They checked into the hotel, had a relaxed lunch, and enjoyed a couple of cold beers before heading out to 'Stezland' for a preliminary look at the house. The property was as rugged as Fergus had remembered, but he and Geoff had come with a plan: a quick walkthrough to start generating ideas for the refurbishment before diving into a full day of design work the next day.

Geoff was immediately struck by the extent of the house's deterioration, but he quickly realised that much of the damage was cosmetic. The wallpapered walls were peeling, and sections of the plasterboard ceiling had fallen in, but nothing that couldn't be fixed with a bit of work. As they moved through the rooms, Geoff began to understand the reasons behind some of the structural issues.

"The ceiling's a mess in places," Geoff noted, "but it looks like the problem is mainly a lack of proper back blocking of joints. The ceiling adhesive's failed, and those cheap-looking pressed metal battens haven't held up."

He was relieved to find that the roof trusses, made from solid Redwood hardwood, were in good shape, with no signs of termite damage. The roof sarking and metal roofing were also in excellent condition, which meant there was no immediate work to be done there. Inside, the timber flooring, made from Australian Spotted Gum, had been carefully laid over a membrane on the concrete slab. Remarkably, it was in pristine condition, needing nothing more than a sanding and a fresh seal to make it look as good as new.

However, the veranda decking was another matter. The treated Hoop Pine bearers had failed, which had caused the Spotted Gum decking to warp and rot.

The external walls and partition walls, constructed from solid 150 and 200 series concrete masonry block, were in superb condition. It was clear that the house had been well-built in many respects, but some issues were too significant to overlook.

"The plumbing's the real issue here," Geoff said as he inspected the pipes. "This HDPE stuff's been eaten by rats in several places. The septic tank has collapsed, and to get power back to the house, we're looking at about eight kilometres of new connections, that's going to be a costly job."

By Saturday night, Geoff had handwritten a comprehensive scope of work and told Fergus that he would type it up and send it over the following week, along with a list of reputable contractors for the job. It had been a productive day, and both men were eager to wind down. They headed to the hotel for dinner and then made their way over to the bowling club, where Geoff was eager to meet Colin Freebody, who was there that evening with his wife, Marge.

As they walked into the club, Fergus couldn't help but feel a sense of anticipation. The next steps for the property were becoming clearer, and with Geoff's expertise, it seemed like they were on the right track. Now, with the evening unfolding, it was time to take a well-earned break and catch up with some old acquaintances.

Before Fergus could bring any tradespeople onto the Stezland property, he faced a significant obstacle: the track that led past the gorge was far too narrow and rough for the heavy machinery and material trucks his contractors would need to bring in. Currently, only a four-wheel-drive utility could make it through, and that simply wouldn't suffice for the scale of the refurbishment he was planning.

To get things moving, Fergus sought quotes for the necessary infrastructure upgrades. The first came from an electrician, who quoted a staggering $23,000 per kilometre to reinstate the power lines and reconnect the house to the grid. This figure covered a single-phase connection from the 'Gatehouse' all the way to the renovated home, which sat several kilometres away.

Next, he sought quotes for upgrading the track itself. The quotes came back at a similar price, with the total cost to upgrade the track running alongside the gorge reaching a comparable $23,000 per kilometre. With several kilometres of track and power lines needing to be done, the total cost for both projects came in at a jaw-dropping $375,000.

Fergus sat back and stared at the figures. There was no way he could justify that kind of expense, especially considering the overall project would already be pushing his budget to the limit. The sheer cost was a dealbreaker, and that's when a thought struck him.

"Why not take matters into my own hands?" he mused. If the existing contractors were charging that much for basic upgrades, perhaps it was time to take control of the civil works himself. Instead of paying a third party for the job, he could start his own civil works company, cutting out the middleman and tackling the infrastructure work on his own terms.

With his background and determination, it was a bold but sensible decision. Fergus didn't shy away from challenges, and this was a challenge he was ready to take on. It was a significant financial commitment, but it would ultimately save him a substantial amount of money in the long run. And with his own civil works company on the ground, he could ensure the quality and timeline of the work were to his exact specifications.

It was time to roll up his sleeves and get to work, starting with transforming the track and the power supply, making Stezland accessible and operational once again.

Fergus decided to reach out to another old army comrade, Tim Abbott, who had been running an earthmoving company based in Yass, New South Wales, the last time they spoke. Fergus left a message on Tim's answering machine, detailing his idea for starting a civil works operation in Far North Queensland. Just as Fergus was about to leave his house in Little Mulgrave to run some errands, the phone rang. It was Tim, sounding genuinely excited to hear from his old mate. The two of them quickly fell into a comfortable conversation, reminiscing about their army days and catching up on each other's lives.

When Fergus finally steered the conversation toward Tim's business, he noticed a hesitation in Tim's voice. After a moment, Tim reluctantly told him that, sadly, his earthmoving business was no longer operational. His wife had left him, and his property in Yass, his home and the land he had worked hard for, was now on the market. Tim admitted he wasn't sure what direction he was going to take next.

Without missing a beat, Fergus immediately suggested that Tim come up to Cairns. "Get on a plane, Tim," he said. "Let's talk about setting up a civil works operation here in the Far North. I could use someone like you."

Tim's tone shifted to one of uncertainty as he explained the difficult situation he was in financially. "I've just paid out my ex-wife for her share of the property," he said. "Right now, I can barely afford a pack of cigarettes, but that should change soon enough, I've got a contract on my place. Once that's all sorted, I'll give you a call."

But Fergus wouldn't hear of it. He wasn't about to let his old mate miss out on an opportunity to start fresh. "Forget about waiting for that contract to close," Fergus insisted. "I'll send you two thousand bucks via the Yass Post Office.

Get yourself sorted and come up here next weekend. I'll make sure you're taken care of when you get here."

Tim, clearly overwhelmed with both gratitude and excitement, didn't hesitate. "I'm on my way," he said, already eager to leave Yass behind and take Fergus up on the offer. They worked out the details, and within two days, Tim would be landing in Cairns, ready to embark on a new chapter of his life, and reconnect with an old friend who had just given him a lifeline.

Fergus hung up the phone feeling a surge of satisfaction. He had no doubt that Tim was the right person to help him get Stezland off the ground, and this collaboration was exactly the kind of fresh start Tim needed. It was a win-win situation.

It was a crisp Friday morning when Fergus picked Tim Abbott up from the airport at 8:30 AM. By 9:00 AM, they were already on their way to Shiptons Flat, and the usual four to five-hour road trip felt like mere minutes. The two old comrades from the RAE (Royal Australian Engineers) quickly fell into easy conversation, reminiscing about their shared experiences in the army. Their laughter and stories filled the car, making the long drive seem effortless.

As they neared their destination, it wasn't until they arrived at the 'Gatehouse' that Fergus began to tell Tim about the plans he had for Stezland, the property he had inherited.

"Starting from this gate here," Fergus said, pointing to the entrance near the house, "I need to turn this track into a proper road all the way down to where we're going. And we'll need to reinstate the power lines that were burnt out a while back."

Tim nodded thoughtfully and reached into the back seat of the vehicle, pulling out a well-worn notebook from his backpack, the only luggage he had brought with him. He opened the notebook and began sketching the track as they drove along, jotting down ideas and measurements.

When they reached Stezland, Tim's reaction was everything Fergus had expected. "Oh, wow, that's some place," he exclaimed, clearly impressed. "And what a location."

Tim spent the next few hours absorbed in the property's vastness and potential. As they made their way back toward the 'Gatehouse,' Tim asked Fergus to stop several times at various points along the track. Each time, he got out of the car, walked along the trail, and made more notes for the road construction and power-line restoration. His mind was already whirring with ideas for how to transform the land into something functional, efficient, and lasting.

After calling in to say hello to Rodney and the others at the 'Gatehouse,' they made their way back to Cairns. They stopped at the Hambledon Hotel in Edmonton for a hearty dinner, exchanging more war stories and catching up on the years that had passed since they last worked together.

Finally, they arrived at Little Mulgrave, where Fergus showed Tim to his room in the house. "Make yourself at home," Fergus said with a grin. "We've got plenty of work ahead of us, but for now, take it easy and settle in."

Tim, feeling both excited and grateful for the fresh start, nodded. He knew this was the opportunity he had been waiting for, and he couldn't wait to get to work on Stezland.

The weekend passed quietly, focused mostly on strategic planning for the road construction. Fergus and Tim spent their time mapping out their equipment needs, determining what machinery would be required to tackle the massive project. The plan was to buy primarily secondhand equipment, aiming to keep costs manageable while still securing the necessary machinery. With a rough budget of around three million dollars, they knew that every purchase needed to be well thought out.

Tim, drawing on his years of experience in the industry, suggested that the best marketplace for sourcing the equipment would be Queensland. "Moving heavy machinery is a logistical nightmare," he explained, "and it's not only time-consuming but also expensive. It makes more sense to source it locally. Plus, buying our own transporter could save us a lot of money in the long run. We could use it to deliver the machinery, and the prime mover could double as a B-double with a tipping body for hauling road materials."

Fergus agreed, impressed by Tim's thorough understanding of the intricacies of the project. On Monday morning, Tim set off for Brisbane to begin the hunt for the necessary equipment. Meanwhile, Fergus turned his attention to securing transportable accommodation for the crew. His plan was to have five units delivered to the 'Gatehouse,' where there was already power available. The accommodation would include kitchen and lunchroom facilities, as well as an office. These units, available for purchase in Cairns, were set to arrive by the following weekend. It was the first step in getting the site ready for the heavy construction work ahead.

With everything coming together, Fergus couldn't help but feel a sense of urgency. He knew his bank balance would soon take a significant hit as they purchased equipment and set up camp. Though the sale of his Canberra property had given him a solid financial cushion, Fergus made the decision to place the Little Mulgrave property on the market. After all, he'd be living in one of the dongas on Stezland once the work began, and the little house at Little Mulgrave would no longer serve his needs. Furthermore, any equipment or personal items he wished to retain could be stored in one of the many sheds on Stezland.

It was all starting to come together for Fergus and his vision of Stezland. The magnitude of the project was beginning to sink in, but he felt ready for the challenge. As the week ahead unfolded, he would need to stay focused and determined, knowing that this would be a journey that would change everything.

Fergus reached out to local Gordonvale real estate agents, Les and Kay Walsh, to discuss the sale of his property. They quickly arranged a property inspection for the following Tuesday morning with Kay. As the conversation unfolded, it became clear that Kay was well-versed in the local market and had a strong sense of the value of properties in the area. Fergus, with his own estimations, had valued his Little Mulgrave property, which boasted a sprawling five-bedroom home, outbuildings, and forty fenced hectares of land, at around one point seven million dollars. He had originally purchased it sixteen years ago for one point two million.

However, Fergus was pleasantly surprised when Kay Walsh suggested listing the property at two point four million dollars, with the expectation of settling around the two to two point two million dollar range. Her confidence in the value of the property gave Fergus a boost, and he agreed to move forward with her plan. Kay also recommended that her husband, Les, inspect the property to get a firsthand look at its condition and potential. Fergus, in turn, told her that he would be available on the coming Friday to facilitate Les's visit.

Later that afternoon, Fergus took care of another important matter. He called Rodney at the 'Gatehouse' using the telephone line that Fergus had arranged to be installed by Telstra. They discussed the logistics for the upcoming Wednesday, when they would begin marking out the location for the work camp. The camp would be situated near the 'Gatehouse,' with access to electricity, but far enough away to ensure Rodney and his group maintained their privacy. It was crucial that the work camp be functional while respecting the boundaries of Rodney's space, and Fergus wanted to make sure everything was in place before any construction began.

As the week unfolded, it was clear that everything was coming together for Fergus. With the potential sale of Little Mulgrave in progress and the groundwork being laid for the Stezland project, the next chapter of his plans was rapidly becoming a reality. While there was still much work ahead, Fergus could sense that his vision for Stezland and the new venture was on the cusp of taking flight.

On Wednesday, the mark-out for the portable buildings went ahead smoothly with the building supply company, Fergus, and Rodney all on-site. Two of the supply company's 'Bobcats' were already working, preparing the area for the installation of the three buildings scheduled for delivery that day. Rodney had arranged for an electrical contractor to be available, ensuring the site was properly equipped for the new installations.

As Fergus was about to leave the property, he noticed a Cooktown Council vehicle approaching. He stopped to see what the matter was. The man in the vehicle was the local building inspector, who informed Fergus that he had been made aware of dwellings being constructed on the property without the proper building permits.

Fergus immediately refuted the claim, explaining that no construction was taking place, but rather, temporary accommodation was being installed, and no permits were required for such structures.

The building inspector, however, didn't take kindly to this response. "It's up to me to decide whether permits are required or not," he snapped, his tone sharp and condescending.

Fergus, who was already growing irritated, felt his old military instincts kicking in. He stepped up his response, his voice firm and commanding. "It's up to me who comes on my property," he said, his tone matching the inspector's. "Now turn around and get off this property, instantly."

The inspector, now visibly taken aback, tried to assert his authority further. "I have the right of entry on any property in this area," he retorted, his tone growing more hostile.

Fergus, no longer willing to entertain the inspector's arrogance, met his gaze with unwavering determination. "Fuck off now and don't come back," he said, his voice steady and cold. "Why do people want to piss me off?" he thought to himself as the inspector, realising he wasn't getting any further with Fergus, turned the council vehicle around and left.

Once the inspector was gone, Fergus made his way back to the 'Gatehouse' to give Rodney a heads-up. He warned him that the inspector might return with the police, but reassured him that he would handle the situation if it arose. With that, Fergus left once again, heading back to Little Mulgrave, his mind still simmering from the confrontation but determined to keep the focus on his growing project.

Les Walsh, like his wife Kay, was thoroughly impressed with the Little Mulgrave property. After a thorough inspection, the couple approached Fergus with a personal offer of two million dollars for the sprawling five-bedroom home and surrounding land. Fergus, without hesitation, verbally accepted their offer, pleased that the sale was moving forward smoothly.

The Walshes explained that they would return later that day with a formal contract for the sale, offering a thirty-day settlement period and a negative commission on the sale, which was a favourable arrangement for Fergus. This meant that he would be able to move into a donga on Stezland as soon as next week, allowing him to begin focusing fully on the Stezland project without the burden of maintaining the Little Mulgrave property.

The week flew by, and by the end of the month, Fergus had indeed relocated to Stezland, settling into a donga while the final steps of the property sale were sorted. The move marked a fresh beginning, and Fergus was excited for the next phase of his venture.

In the meantime, Tim Abbott had returned to deliver a Caterpillar 336DL excavator, which was hauled by a 1988 second-hand Mack Superliner Mark II and a transport low loader quad axle. Tim had purchased the equipment at an auction in Brisbane and registered it under Fergus's new company, Stezland Civil and Earthmoving Contractors Proprietary Limited.

After unloading the excavator, Fergus joined Tim in the low loader, and the two of them set off for Brisbane to collect another Mack prime mover with a tipping body. This truck was carrying two Bobcat wheeled skid steer loaders, which Fergus would drive back to Shiptons Flat. Tim, meanwhile, was to collect a Cat 140M Road Grader with the low loader and bring it back to Stezland.

Fergus left Brisbane a day earlier than Tim, as the grader was not ready to travel on the same schedule. After driving for twelve hours, and in line with Queensland Motor Transport regulations for heavy vehicles, Fergus stopped at Fairview, a small town near Mackay, for the night. The local motel catered specifically to heavy vehicles, making it a convenient stop for truckers.

The next morning, while fuelling up at the Fairview service station and enjoying an early breakfast, Fergus struck up a conversation with a man who appeared to be roughly his own age. The man, with a noticeable accent, introduced himself as "Everyone calls me Wes," though his full name turned out to be Werner Fischer. Wes explained that he had been driving a truck from Brisbane to Innisfail when the vehicle had caught fire the previous day. Now, he was making his way back to Tully, a small town just south of Innisfail, to collect another truck to drive to Adelaide.

Without hesitation, Fergus offered Wes a lift to Tully, knowing that he could use some company during the long drive and that the offer would help out the stranded trucker. Wes gratefully accepted, and the two men set off together, exchanging stories and building a quick rapport during the journey.

Wes settled comfortably into the passenger seat, his large frame making the space seem even more compact. He looked over at Fergus with a mischievous grin and said, "Yar und I von't be grinding off the gearing as you are," his accent thick but clearly joking.

Fergus burst into laughter at the comment, shaking his head. "Mate, you're more than welcome to drive," he said with a grin. "I haven't even got a license to drive this fucker; this is my first time behind the wheel of a truck."

Wes laughed too, his deep chuckles rumbling in the quiet cabin. "You are lucky you have come this far," he said, shaking his head in disbelief. "Do you even have a car driver's license?"

Fergus nodded, though he felt a little sheepish. "Yeah, I do. Why?"

Wes leaned back and smiled. "Well, a car license also works as a permit to learn how to drive a truck, so long as there's a licensed truck driver in the vehicle giving instruction."

Fergus exhaled in relief, the tension that had been building up in his chest easing. "Well, that's a relief," he admitted, feeling much more comfortable now. "I was planning to sort it out when I get back to Cooktown, but I guess I can wait."

Wes nodded and chuckled. "No need to worry, mate. You're driving just fine."

As the miles passed, Wes asked about the two Bobcats loaded on the back of the truck. Fergus explained the project at Stezland, describing the work that needed to be done to make an access road for renovations and to re-establish the power lines to the house. Wes's interest piqued as Fergus spoke.

"I tell you, Fergus," Wes began, his voice growing more animated, "I've operated those American Bobcats before I joined the army. I did a lot of road and bridge construction, earthworks, dams, drains, you name it. I've seen it all." He paused, looking out the window before continuing. "I moved to Australia after I left the army. I had a sponsorship from some friends of my father's who live in Melbourne."

Fergus listened intently, impressed. "So, you're saying you have experience with all this heavy equipment?"

Wes grinned and shook his head. "Oh, yeah. But fuck Melbourne," he said with a chuckle. "It's colder than Austria, and they don't even recognise my certificates to operate the machinery I worked with back in Germany. So now I'm driving trucks instead."

Fergus couldn't believe his luck. This was exactly the kind of person he needed for the Stezland project, someone with the right skills and a can-do attitude. Without hesitating, he turned to Wes and said, "Well, mate, how would you feel about joining Tim and me up at Stezland? We could use someone like you on the team."

Wes raised an eyebrow, clearly intrigued. "Yeah? That sounds like a good move," he said, a smile creeping onto his face. "But I'll need to go back to Tully, grab my stuff, and tell my boss I'm finished driving for him."

Fergus nodded, understanding the need to wrap things up on Wes's end. "You've got time for that. No rush, mate. We can sort everything when we get back to Tully."

Wes nodded again, looking out at the road ahead, clearly already making plans in his head. "Alright, mate, I'm in. Let's do it."

During the trip to Tully, Fergus learned more about Wes's background, which only deepened his respect for the man. Wes revealed that he had served in the German Armed Forces' elite Special Operations Command (Kommando Spezialkräfte, KSK), and had left the service holding the rank of Hauptmann. Fergus, having served in the Australian Army, immediately made the comparison to the Australian SAS and was impressed. Hauptmann was equivalent to an Australian Army Captain, just one rank below Fergus's own, and this shared experience, combined with Wes's distinguished service, elevated his standing in Fergus's eyes.

Wes's calm, assured demeanour, coupled with his military experience, was clearly a great find. Fergus found that they had an easy rapport, and it was clear that Wes wasn't just a capable operator when it came to machinery and heavy trucks, he had also seen his fair share of challenges and had come out on top. It felt like fate that their paths had crossed.

By the time they reached Tully, their first stop was the trucking company where Wes had been employed. The company's owners expressed their sadness over his departure, but there was no animosity. They wished him well and assured him that if things didn't work out, his old job would be waiting for him. It was a good sign that Wes had left on such amicable terms.

Next, they drove to Wes's rented unit in Tully Heads. His belongings, though not many, included a 1975 SWB FJ Landcruiser with a canvas top. However, the Landcruiser was unregistered, which posed a problem for getting it up to Stezland. As they unloaded the rest of his belongings, Fergus's mind began working on a solution.

"I've got an idea," Fergus said, turning to Wes. "Let's hold off on getting your cruiser registered for now. Tim's coming through this way tomorrow, likely just before midday. We can wait on the highway, and when he comes by, we can fit your Landcruiser onto the low loader with the grader. It'll save us the trouble of getting it sorted out separately. We can also load the rest of your stuff into the Mack's sleeper cab, make it all easy."

Wes nodded, impressed by the idea. "Good thinking, mate. That'll work perfectly." It was clear to both of them that, despite the unforeseen circumstances of Wes's situation, things were starting to fall into place. With the plan set, they knew they'd be able to get everything to Stezland without much hassle and start putting together the team that would take on the huge task ahead.

After spending a restful night at a motel in Tully, which offered truck parking and a hearty meal, Fergus was in good spirits. He and Wes had enjoyed a great evening together, sharing stories over drinks. Wes, being a teetotaler, had stuck to water, but his company was just as enjoyable, and the night passed quickly. Fergus's estimate on Tim's arrival time in Tully turned out to be spot on. He had managed to contact Tim by CB radio some distance before Tully, guiding him to the Tully Heads turnoff.

By the time Tim rolled in, there was plenty of room at the roadside to park the low loader and Mack Superliner. Tim was introduced to Wes, and Fergus explained that Wes would be joining the crew at Stezland. Tim seemed pleased with the addition, recognising that it would give them the manpower to efficiently complete the tasks at hand, especially since Wes had experience with both heavy machinery and roadwork. With the addition of Wes, it meant that both trucks would be able to make the return trip to Brisbane to pick up more equipment, another solid step forward in their operation.

The drive from Tully to Shiptons Flat took a little under seven hours. By the time the trucks arrived at the 'Gatehouse' and the dongas that evening, it was already around 7:00 PM. The plan was to unload the trucks the next morning, but for now, they decided to take a well-deserved break. They made the quick decision to drive the fifty kilometres into Cooktown for dinner, a small town they had all come to appreciate. Wes, being the only one sober, was designated the driver for the evening.

Fergus and Tim were happy to let Wes take the wheel, knowing it meant they could enjoy a few beers over dinner without worrying about who would drive back. The evening in Cooktown turned into a light-hearted affair, and the two of them did more than just eat, they brought back a healthy supply of cold beer in stubbies to the 'Gatehouse' so they could enjoy a few more drinks once they were back. There was a feeling of camaraderie, a new chapter unfolding with the addition of Wes to the team, and everything seemed to be coming together nicely at Stezland.

The next morning, after unloading both trucks, Fergus and Tim spent the day preparing their machines for the return trip to Brisbane. They checked the Caterpillar D7 bulldozer, which was set to be loaded onto the low loader, and discussed the details of the equipment they would be collecting next. In addition to the bulldozer, there was the air track rock drilling machine and a wheeled compressor, both of which would be placed on a flat-top trailer that they had yet to source in Brisbane. This trailer would be towed by the second Mack truck, which would leave its tipping body behind at Stezland for the time being.

With everything planned, there wasn't much left for Fergus to do until Tim and Wes returned with the next batch of equipment. He focused on getting the dongas and office set up, ensuring the site was operational. Fergus also arranged for a telephone line to be connected, which was essential for communications, and he took the opportunity to familiarise himself with some of the growing list of machinery now scattered about four hundred meters from the 'Gatehouse'.

Feeling the need for a break from the logistics, Fergus decided to take a drive past the 'Gatehouse' and follow the left-hand fork in the track that led towards the higher ranges. He was in search of a potential quarry site for road base materials. As he drove, he noticed that the colour of the track shifted to a darker red, signalling a change in the terrain. It seemed damp, though it was as dry as the rest of the land. Curiosity piqued, he followed the track until it veered left, leading him to a rough patch of rising ground that became too steep for his vehicle to ascend.

Determined to investigate further, Fergus grabbed his mattock and pick from the truck and set off on foot towards the promising area of red material. As he dug small samples, he found the ground to be rich in decomposed granite. It seemed abundant and relatively easy to extract. He figured he could bring the Caterpillar excavator out the following day to perform a few test digs to confirm his findings.

However, as he made his way back to the donga camp, he was surprised to find the building inspector from the Cooktown Shire walking around the site, clipboard in hand, accompanied by a police officer. The sight instantly put Fergus on alert. The inspector was taking notes, presumably in response to the concerns raised about the temporary accommodation being set up without proper permits.

Fergus's blood began to boil. The inspector had already given him trouble once before, and now it seemed he was back, this time with law enforcement in tow. It looked like Fergus's earlier warning to Rodney about a possible police visit had come true. He took a deep breath, mentally preparing himself for yet another confrontation. This time, he was ready. He just needed to stay calm, make sure he had all the necessary details on hand, and handle this the right way. No more unnecessary drama. The inspector wasn't going to stop him from getting this project off the ground.

As Fergus approached the inspector and the police officer, he could feel his patience starting to wear thin. He took a steadying breath and asked, "What can I do for you guys?"

The inspector began to speak, introducing himself, "I'm the building inspector for Cooktown, "

Fergus cut him off sharply, his irritation starting to show. "I know who you are. What do you want out here?"

The inspector, unfazed, continued, "Do you have a permit for these build, "

Before he could finish, Fergus interrupted again, his voice rising. "I've told you already, these are temporary structures. The company I'm renting them from has told me no permits are required. Now, get off my property!"

Fergus's tone grew more agitated as he spoke, his frustration with the situation mounting. The police officer, sensing the tension, stepped in. "This man is only doing his job, you can speak to him in a civilised manner."

Fergus spun to face the officer, his voice a mixture of anger and disbelief. "And who the fuck are you? And what the fuck do you want?" His good mood was quickly slipping away, and the old, authoritative version of himself, the Major, started to emerge again.

The police officer, unfazed, responded coldly, "I am Senior Constable Kirkland, and you will show some respect, or, "

Fergus, cutting him off, responded with a sharp tone, "Orr…fucking what? ….YOU… introduce yourself….. FIRST next time. Then tell me what you're doing here."

He took a step closer to the officer, his gaze intense. "You don't just butt into a conversation that has nothing to do with you. And you definitely don't come on my property without prior consent. Do you understand?"

Kirkland smirked, unfazed by the threat. "I've had dealings with you before, haven't I?" He paused, looking at Fergus with a hint of recognition. "Driving with over the prescribed blood alcohol limit, if I remember correctly."

Fergus shot back, his voice dripping with sarcasm, "Well, I thought it was speeding and a vehicle defect."

Kirkland's smirk faded slightly, but he continued, "Actually, all three. But I decided to let you off."

Fergus wasn't having it. "Because you're a fool or just too gutless?" he snapped, his anger clearly rising.

The constable opened his mouth, but thought better of it, closing it without a word. He turned to the building inspector and said, "I would seem that you should be talking to the owners of these buildings and not the lessee. It's time to go."

With that, the constable climbed into his car without so much as a glance toward Fergus, pulling away without a word. The inspector, now looking increasingly uncomfortable, started to get into his car, but then hesitated. He rolled down his window and called out, "Who owns the buildings?"

Fergus turned to watch the police car retreat, feeling a surge of satisfaction. "Who owns the buildings? PLEASE," he muttered under his breath as he walked away. He wasn't going to indulge the inspector any further. "Fuck you," he thought to himself, a bitter smile on his face. As he walked back toward his donga, he couldn't shake the feeling that there was something off about this local cop. Mitchell had been right, this was the same officer involved in the death of Amelia.

Once back at the 'Gatehouse,' Fergus called the Cooktown Caltex dealer from the telephone, taking a moment to calm himself with a cold beer provided by Rodney. He inquired about a diesel tank on a stand and asked if they had any second-hand diesel tankers. They didn't need to be registered; he simply needed something to use on his property.

The dealer promised to deliver a 10,000-litre tank the following morning. True to their word, the tank was delivered just after lunch and filled with diesel, ready for use on Stezland. Despite the tension with the inspector and police, things were beginning to fall into place for Fergus. He just had to stay focused on his goals and navigate the increasingly complicated local dynamics.

Fergus filled the excavator's fuel tank, started the engine, and began the slow, deliberate trek toward the Deco site he had scouted the day before. The journey, though only a few kilometres, took over an hour due to the rough and uneven terrain. Despite the bumpy ride, Fergus was optimistic. He had high hopes for this site, it seemed to have an abundant supply of decomposed granite, perfect for the road base they needed.

Upon arriving, Fergus manoeuvred the big Cat excavator into position and began digging into the side of the hill. Clearing the vegetation was the first step, and once that was done, the real work began. To his satisfaction, the granite beneath the surface broke apart with relative ease. The material looked promising, but as he worked, Fergus realised that while it was loose enough to extract, they would need a portable crushing plant to refine it into a suitable consistency for road base. Another piece of equipment to add to the growing list.

On the way back to camp, Fergus's mind was a whirlwind of thoughts. He mentally reviewed the endless list of equipment and supplies they still needed: a crushing plant, a water tanker, a road roller... The list felt like it would never end. Each new solution brought another challenge, and he couldn't help but wonder, "Where does it end?"

Back at the office donga, Fergus was relieved to find that the phone line had finally been connected. Wasting no time, he made several calls to equipment suppliers. His first big win came when he found a transportable crushing plant in Mount Isa. The seller assured Fergus that they could have it delivered and operational within two weeks. One more box ticked, he thought, feeling a small sense of accomplishment.

Next, he located an ideal water tanker in Cardwell, a Kenworth eight-wheeler with twin steer axles, originally a concrete truck, but now fitted with a flat eight-meter-long body. It carried a 6,000-litre water tank at the rear and a 2,000-litre diesel tank up front. The truck was fully registered and roadworthy, making it perfect for their needs. Fergus arranged for Tim and Wes to pick it up over the coming weekend. Another piece of the puzzle falling into place.

The New March

As Fergus approached the camp, he noticed with satisfaction that both of their trucks had returned from Brisbane. Tim and Wes were already at work, unloading the Caterpillar D7 bulldozer. The air track rock drill and compressor, loaded onto the other truck, would need a ramp for unloading. Fortunately, the dozer would be the perfect tool to build it.

He parked the excavator nearby and walked over to join Tim and Wes. The sight of the two trucks, fully loaded with heavy machinery, gave Fergus a renewed sense of purpose. They were making progress, and despite the constant hurdles, he was determined to see this project through. Every challenge they overcame brought them one step closer to transforming Stezland into a fully operational site.

As they began discussing plans for the next few days, Fergus couldn't help but smile. They were well on their way, and with Tim and Wes by his side, things were finally starting to come together.

After unloading the equipment, the crew cleaned up and unanimously agreed to head into Cooktown for dinner and drinks at the RSL club, though not necessarily in that order. The long day of physical labor had left them all famished, and the thought of a hearty meal combined with a few cold beers was the perfect way to unwind.

The Cooktown RSL didn't disappoint. They enjoyed a fantastic meal, accompanied by easy camaraderie and laughter as they discussed their plans for the weekend, particularly the upcoming trip to Cardwell to collect the twin-steer Kenworth. Fergus mentioned that he had made all the necessary arrangements and was confident the truck would be ready for pick-up by Saturday morning.

During the conversation, Fergus proudly showed off his new Nokia mobile phone. The sleek device was the latest in communication technology, and though impressive, it quickly became a subject of lighthearted mockery when they discovered there was no mobile service in the Cooktown area yet.

"Looks great, Fergus," Tim said, grinning. "But until there's actual service out here, it's basically a very expensive paperweight."

Fergus laughed, acknowledging the truth in Tim's words. "Yeah, pretty useless for now, but it does have this neat recording feature that works without service," he said, demonstrating how to record and play back audio. Despite its lack of practicality in the region, the phone sparked a brief conversation about the future of communication. They all agreed it could be a game-changer someday, even if, for now, it was too large to fit in a pocket and had to be carried around by hand.

By the time they wrapped up dinner and a few rounds of drinks, it was close to 11:30 p.m. They spilled out of the club into the cool night air, feeling relaxed and content. Wes, who had stuck to Coke all evening, took the driver's seat of Fergus's trusty Land Rover while the others piled in. The streets of Cooktown were quiet at this hour, and the drive back to camp promised to be a peaceful one.

As Wes navigated the familiar route back toward Shiptons Flat, Fergus leaned back in his seat, reflecting on how far things had come in just a short time. With a capable team, a growing fleet of equipment, and progress underway, he felt a growing sense of optimism. Sure, there was still a mountain of work ahead, but nights like these, good food, good company, and shared plans, reminded him why it was all worth it.

They had just left Hope Street, where it turned into the Mulligan Highway, and the speed limit increased from sixty to eighty kilometres per hour. As Wes smoothly accelerated from sixty to eighty, a set of blinding high beams, accompanied by flashing blue lights, sped up behind them. Without hesitation, Wes slowed the Land Rover and looked for a safe spot to pull over. The police vehicle followed closely behind and stopped as well. Fergus, sensing trouble, discreetly switched on the recording feature of his new Nokia phone, which was sitting on the centre console.

A figure carrying a flashlight approached from the right side, its beam cutting through the darkness. The voice that accompanied the light was all too familiar.
"Well, well... if it isn't Mr. Laird," sneered Senior Constable Stanley Kirkland, his tone dripping with malice. "You won't be getting out of this one tonight... Wait, who the fuck are you?" His smug confidence faltered as the flashlight illuminated the face of the driver.

Wes remained calm, offering a polite but firm response. "I'm Wes, mate. What can I do for you?"

Kirkland's face contorted in confusion. For a moment, he appeared unsure if he had pulled over the wrong vehicle. Then, recognising Fergus in the passenger seat, he recomposed himself, clearly irritated.

"Any reason you're doing eighty in a sixty zone?" Kirkland asked, the accusation sharp and accusatory.

"I was doing sixty in the sixty zone and just getting up to eighty in the eighty zone," Wes replied evenly.

"Don't get fucking smart with me, pal. You were doing eighty in the sixty zone. Let me see your license," Kirkland barked.

Without hesitation, Wes leaned forward, reaching behind him to retrieve his wallet from his back pocket. Before he could even bring it out, the situation escalated dramatically. In an instant, Kirkland's hand went to his holster, and suddenly the cold muzzle of a police-issued Glock was pressed against Wes's neck.

"Freeze! One more move and you're dead! Put both hands on the steering wheel, now, very, very slowly," Kirkland shouted, his voice shrill, shaking with excitement but lacking any real authority.

"Whoa, whoa, hey, put the gun down!" Fergus yelled, his voice filled with alarm.

"Mein Gott! I'm only getting my license! Vhat is mit you?" Wes exclaimed in disbelief, his German accent pronounced under the stress of the moment.

Despite the weapon pressed to his neck, Wes remained unnervingly calm. Fergus noticed how his new friend hadn't even flinched. What happened next was almost too quick to process, like something out of a well-rehearsed action sequence. In one fluid motion, Wes disarmed Kirkland, his hand snapping out to grab the Glock before twisting it out of the officer's grip. The entire encounter lasted less than a second, and before anyone could react, Wes was holding the weapon.

For a tense moment, everything was still. Wes's eyes were locked on Kirkland, cold and calculating. He could have easily taken Kirkland down completely, could have ended the encounter far more violently, but he didn't. Instead, he lowered the weapon, holding it at his side, his expression more annoyed than aggressive.

Kirkland's mouth opened and closed as if trying to form words, but nothing coherent came out. The humiliation was evident on his face as he realised he had been effortlessly overpowered.

"Mein Gott," Wes said again, shaking his head in disbelief. "I vas just getting my license, and you pull a gun on me? Is this normal police behaviour here?"

Fergus, still processing what had just happened, took a deep breath and regained his composure. "What the hell is wrong with you, Kirkland? You nearly got yourself killed over nothing."

The blood had drained from Kirkland's face, leaving him pale and motionless, as if frozen in shock. Wes, moving with the same calm efficiency he had shown when disarming the constable, opened his door, stepped out, and grabbed hold of Kirkland. Without a hint of malice but with firm control, he spun the shaken officer around and pressed him over the bonnet of the Land Rover.

"Cool… cool. Be cool, und you vill be OK," Wes said in a measured tone, his voice carrying both reassurance and authority.

Fergus stepped out and approached, his expression grim. "What the hell is wrong with this copper, Wes?" Wes shrugged, keeping Kirkland securely pinned.

"I don't know," Fergus muttered, his mind racing. "But this has gone way too far. We need to call the police in Cairns or Mareeba and report this mess. Wes, see if you can find his handcuffs. Tim, go turn off his car and lock it."

Tim, visibly unsettled but following Fergus's lead, walked over to the patrol car. He switched off the engine, pocketed the keys, and locked the doors before returning to the Land Rover.

Meanwhile, Wes found Kirkland's handcuffs on his belt and deftly snapped them onto his wrists behind his back. With a firm grip, he guided the disgraced officer toward the back seat of the Land Rover. Kirkland didn't resist, still too dazed to mount any real protest.

They placed him in the back seat, right next to Tim, who immediately recoiled as a foul stench filled the vehicle. "Oh, come on!" Tim groaned, his face twisted in disgust. "He crapped himself! You're kidding me, right?"

Fergus, standing by the open door, caught a whiff and grimaced. "Great. Just great." He looked at Tim apologetically. "Sorry, mate, but you'll have to deal with it for now. We can't exactly strap him to the roof rack."

Tim reluctantly climbed in, leaning as far away from Kirkland as possible and pressing his head almost completely out of the window for fresh air. Wes climbed back into the driver's seat, and Fergus got into the front passenger seat, exhaling sharply as he tried to think through their next move.

As the Land Rover began moving again, Kirkland seemed to regain some of his composure. His initial fear morphed into bluster, and he started to mutter threats under his breath. "You're all going to prison for this. You hear me? Kidnapping a police officer is a serious offence. You're finished, every last one of you."

Fergus turned in his seat, fixing Kirkland with a cold glare. "If I were you, I'd keep quiet, or we'll gag you. We're already doing you a favour by not leaving you handcuffed to your own patrol car."

Kirkland opened his mouth to respond but thought better of it. He clamped his mouth shut, his face flushed with a mix of anger and embarrassment. Fergus turned back around, satisfied that, for the moment, the constable would behave.

Tim, meanwhile, continued to grumble under his breath. "Next time, I'm sitting in the front, no questions asked. This guy stinks like a sewer."

Fergus allowed himself a brief smirk before refocusing. "We'll head back to camp for now. Once we're there, we'll call the regional police and explain what happened. No way this guy should be left roaming around with a badge and a gun."

Wes nodded as he navigated the winding road. "Ja, und ve can record everything, keep it legal, ja? But ve must be careful. This Kirkland, he is dangerous, I can feel it."

Fergus agreed. There was something deeply wrong about Kirkland's behaviour tonight, and it was clear that the constable was not acting like a professional lawman. This wasn't a simple traffic stop gone wrong, there was a deeper problem here, one that likely tied into what Mitchell had mentioned about Kirkland's involvement in Amelia's death.

As they continued their drive, Fergus couldn't help but feel a growing sense of foreboding. Trouble seemed to follow him, and now, with Kirkland in the back seat, stinking up the vehicle and muttering about legal repercussions, that trouble was becoming dangerously real.

At the camp, Fergus flipped through the pages of the phone book, searching for the nearest police station. Tim, leaning against the counter, watched him with a frown. "I wouldn't bother calling anyone nearby. They're probably in cahoots with Cooktown. If Kirkland's got friends in the local precinct, we'll just be handing him back without getting anywhere. Better to call Cairns, more distance, more accountability."

Fergus nodded, realising Tim had a point. It was already past midnight, 12:30 a.m. to be exact, but this wasn't something they could put off until morning. He picked up the phone and dialled the Cairns police station.

"Cairns Police, Constable Wood speaking," came a steady voice on the other end.

"Ahh, Constable..." Fergus hesitated for a moment, unsure of how best to explain the bizarre situation. "We've had an incident near Cooktown, and... well, we've had to make a citizen's arrest on a senior police constable. He's currently being held at a property near Shiptons Flat."

There was a brief pause. Then, "Just a minute," Wood replied curtly. The line went silent, and Fergus felt a growing sense of unease. He considered hanging up and trying again, but before he could act, a different, gruffer voice came on the line.

"What's your location? Are you armed? Can a helicopter land there? How many people are with you? Stay on this line and do not hang up."

The questions came rapid-fire, catching Fergus off guard. He quickly provided the details they asked for, his voice steady despite the tension he felt.

After what seemed like an eternity of silence, the voice returned. "We're sending a team. They'll be there in twenty minutes. Go to an open area, take the police constable with you, and lie face down on the ground. Do not look up at the police, and remain motionless at all times until directed. Do you understand?"

"Yes, we understand," Fergus confirmed, though he felt a strange sense of disbelief at the surreal instructions. The line clicked, signalling the end of the call.

He relayed the message to Wes and Tim, who both exchanged wary glances. "Face down on the ground? Seems a bit over the top, don't you think?" Tim muttered.

"Better safe than sorry," Fergus replied grimly. "We're dealing with a rogue cop. The Cairns team probably doesn't want to take any chances."

They prepared themselves quickly. Kirkland, still handcuffed and now stripped of his trousers, an effort to minimise any threat he might pose, remained unusually silent. He refused to make eye contact with any of them, his face set in a stubborn scowl.

As they led him outside to the designated open area, Wes glanced over at Fergus. "This is insane. I've seen some crazy things in the military, but arresting a cop and calling in a helicopter? This is a first."

"No kidding," Fergus muttered. "Let's just get through this in one piece."

The night air was cool and eerily quiet as they positioned themselves in the clearing, lying face down as instructed. Kirkland was placed a few meters away, his hands still bound behind his back, silent and brooding. Tim grumbled under his breath about the indignity of lying in the dirt, but Fergus shot him a quick look to keep quiet.

Minutes passed in tense silence, each one stretching longer than the last. The only sound was the occasional rustle of the wind through the nearby trees. Then, faintly at first, the low hum of rotor blades began to cut through the stillness, growing louder with each passing second. The police helicopter was approaching.

"Here they come," Wes murmured.

Fergus didn't reply. He kept his head down, hands flat against the ground, heart pounding as the sound of the helicopter grew deafening. Dust and loose leaves swirled around them as the aircraft hovered above, its searchlight sweeping the area in a bright, blinding arc.

Voices shouted over the noise, commanding them to remain still. Moments later, the sound of boots hitting the ground signalled the arrival of the police team. Armed officers surrounded them swiftly, their weapons drawn but steady.

"Stay down! Do not move!" one of the officers barked.

Fergus remained completely still, as did Wes and Tim. Within moments, they were frisked, and their hands were secured with cable ties. Kirkland was also secured, though Fergus noted with some satisfaction that he didn't receive any special treatment despite his former status as a police constable.

Once they were fully restrained, they were pulled to their feet one by one. Fergus kept his expression neutral, watching as the officers methodically assessed the situation.

"Who's in charge here?" an authoritative voice called out. One of the officers, a sergeant by the look of him, stepped forward.

Fergus cleared his throat. "That would be me. Fergus Laird."

The sergeant gave him a measured look, then turned to his team. "Get these three over to the staging area. We'll process the constable separately." He pointed to Kirkland, who was now glaring daggers at Fergus.

"Looks like things are about to get interesting," Fergus muttered under his breath. Whatever happened next, he knew they were in for a long night.

Rough hands forced them face down onto the ground before snapping handcuffs tightly around their wrists. Without explanation, black fabric hoods were pulled over their heads, cutting off their sight and muffling the sounds around them. Disoriented, they were half-dragged, half-marched to a waiting helicopter. The rhythmic thump of the rotors grew louder as they were loaded aboard, pressed into seats, and secured.

The flight didn't seem that long, the hum of the engines droning in their ears while none of them spoke. Bound, hooded, and uncertain of what awaited them, tension hung thick in the air. When the helicopter landed, they were escorted out, still blinded by the hoods, and led into an unknown building.

Inside, they were stripped of their clothing and subjected to a thorough search before being handed paper overalls. Shackles were clamped around their ankles, and they were seated on cold, unforgiving metal chairs. Only then were their hoods removed, leaving them blinking in the harsh fluorescent light.

The room was bare and utilitarian, unpainted concrete block walls, a matching concrete ceiling and floor, and a lingering chill that made the paper overalls feel thin and inadequate. Two armed officers, clad in black tactical uniforms and wielding Heckler & Koch MP5 rifles, flanked the room, their faces hidden behind hoods. At the centre of it all, behind a large, imposing desk, sat a high-ranking police officer in a neatly pressed uniform, flanked by two men in dark suits.

"Start talking," the uniformed officer commanded, his eyes sharp as they swept across the trio. His tone left no room for negotiation.

Fergus, with occasional input from Tim and Wes, carefully recounted the events leading up to Kirkland's arrest. As they spoke, the two suited men scribbled notes furiously in their notebooks, pausing only to exchange brief glances when certain details caught their attention.

When Fergus finished, the officer leaned forward, his expression hard. "Which one of you disarmed the constable?" he demanded.

"I did," Wes said calmly, his voice steady. "I believed my life was in danger, so I neutralised the threat."

The officer's brow furrowed slightly. "What kind of training do you have that allows you to 'neutralise' threats so efficiently?"

"I was an officer in the German Armed Forces, Special Operations Command, Kommando Spezialkräfte, KSK," Wes replied. The mention of the elite unit caused both plainclothes men to glance at each other meaningfully.

One of them, setting down his pen, asked, "Isn't that comparable to the U.S. Navy SEALs?"

Wes shrugged, a faint grin tugging at the corner of his mouth. "Ja, I believe so, only better trained than the Americans." His grin was contagious, briefly lightening the otherwise tense atmosphere as even the interrogators shared a small chuckle.

Fergus, remembering the mobile phone he had used to record Kirkland's approach, spoke up. "I had my mobile phone recording the entire encounter. It was in my hand when we were arrested. I assume you found it?"

The uniformed officer nodded. "Yes, we retrieved the phone. We've listened to the recording. It corroborates much of what you've told us. The phone will be returned to you, minus the recording, which has been deleted for operational reasons."

Fergus frowned slightly but didn't argue. Instead, he shifted his tone. "I'd like to call my lawyer."

"That won't be necessary," the officer said, his tone softening just a fraction. "None of you are being charged with anything. You're free to leave once you sign a confidentiality agreement stating that you won't speak to anyone about what has transpired here. Additionally, we'll provide you with travel warrants for flights back to Cooktown."

Tim, who had remained silent up to this point, finally spoke. "You're not charging us, but you called in a SWAT team, threw us into a chopper in the middle of the night, and put us through this circus? Seems a bit over the top."

The officer's face remained impassive. "We take any perceived threats to our officers very seriously. Our response may seem dramatic to you, but protocol dictates that we act decisively in situations involving potential assaults on law enforcement personnel."

He leaned back slightly, signalling that the debrief was nearly over. "As for your camp, a team conducted a search last night. Several firearms were seized and are currently being held at the Cooktown police station. They can be reclaimed upon presentation of the proper firearms licenses."

Fergus clenched his jaw but kept his composure. He exchanged glances with Tim and Wes before giving a curt nod. "Fine. We'll sign your papers, collect our things, and leave."

The officer gestured toward one of the suited men, who produced a set of documents. As they read through the confidentiality agreements and signed their names, Fergus couldn't help but reflect on the absurdity of the night. They had been pulled into a whirlwind of bureaucracy and paranoia, all because of one crooked cop's vendetta.

When the final signatures were collected, the officer stood and offered a curt, formal nod. "You'll be escorted to a holding area where you can wait for your flight. The matter is now closed. Good luck, gentlemen."

As they were led out of the room, Wes leaned toward Fergus, whispering just loud enough for only him and Tim to hear. "This country is more exciting than I expected."

Fergus chuckled quietly, despite himself. "Welcome to Australia, mate."

It was just coming light at 5:30 a.m. when they emerged from the police station, exhausted but relieved to be free. The air was cool, carrying the faint scent of salt from the nearby ocean. After a few minutes of quiet walking, they spotted a twenty-four-hour café with warm lights spilling out onto the street. The trio stepped inside, grateful for the promise of hot coffee and a brief reprieve from the strange night they'd endured.

As they settled into a booth, sipping their steaming mugs, the weight of the events began to sink in. They had no idea what would happen to Kirkland, no answers, no explanations, just a vague sense that they were being watched.

"The man's a fucking idiot," Fergus muttered, breaking the silence as he stirred his coffee with unnecessary force. His tone carried more than just frustration, it was laced with something deeper.

Wes, ever observant, tilted his head slightly and fixed Fergus with a curious stare. "I am thinking there is more to this man Kirkland, yah? He seems to mean much more to you than just being a crooked cop. Perhaps... you have a hatred for this person?"

Fergus sighed, setting his spoon down with a soft clink. He hadn't intended to unburden himself, but after everything that had happened, it seemed inevitable. Slowly, he began recounting the story of his late wife, Amelia, and the tragic series of events that had led to her death. He explained how Kirkland had harassed both him and his brother Mitchell in the months following her passing, pulling them over without cause and showing up unannounced at the camp just days ago.

As Fergus spoke, Tim listened intently, a frown forming on his face. When Fergus finished, Wes leaned back in his chair, his expression thoughtful but dark.

"If it were me, I would have removed this man a long time ago," Wes said, his tone matter-of-fact and devoid of emotion.

Tim's eyebrows shot up. "It seems you don't fuck around, Wes. The way you stayed calm when that prick shoved a gun to your head? Before I even realised what was happening, you had disarmed him. I wouldn't mess with you, my friend."

Wes grinned slightly but shrugged as if it were nothing. "Calm is everything. Panic gets you killed. Besides, Kirkland was sloppy. He should never have drawn his weapon if he wasn't ready to use it."

Fergus couldn't help but smile at Wes's confidence. Despite the chaos, he was beginning to feel that, with Tim and Wes by his side, they might just be able to push through whatever trouble lay ahead. Still, the lingering question of Kirkland's fate weighed on him. The man was dangerous, but now Fergus had to wonder: just how deep did Kirkland's connections go?

"I'm not sure this is over," Fergus said after a pause. "Kirkland might be out of the picture for now, but I doubt he's gone for good."

Wes gave a slight nod, his gaze sharpening. "If he comes back, we will be ready. I don't believe in leaving unfinished business."

Tim clapped Wes on the back, chuckling softly. "Well, I'll say one thing, you're one hell of a guy to have in a fight."

The mood lightened slightly, and for a brief moment, the trio enjoyed the comfort of hot food and warm company. Yet beneath the surface, all three of them knew that this was only a temporary lull in what was becoming a much larger battle. And as Fergus finished his coffee, he resolved that if Kirkland, or anyone else, came after them again, they wouldn't be caught off guard.

The café was quiet as they sat with their toasted sandwiches and steaming mugs of coffee. Tim took a long sip before casually suggesting, "You know, since we're already three-quarters of the way to Cardwell, I might as well head over and pick up the twin-steer truck. There's a Greyhound bus running this morning, and I should be back at camp by tonight."

Fergus and Wes exchanged a glance, then nodded in agreement. It made sense. As long as Tim could manage to stay awake after their long, eventful night, it would save time. With a plan in place, they finished their breakfast, paid the bill, and parted ways, Tim headed for the bus station while Fergus and Wes made their way to the Cairns airport to catch a flight on the Dash 8 service to Cooktown.

Once they landed in Cooktown, Fergus pulled out his phone and called Rodney, who was more than willing to come and collect them from the small airport. By the time Rodney arrived, the morning sun was casting long shadows across the tarmac. Fergus and Wes were standing outside the airport shed, waiting.

As soon as Rodney pulled up, he jumped out of his car and launched into a barrage of questions. "What the fuck is going on? We heard helicopters last night, then police sirens blaring through the bush. This morning, two constables showed up at the Gatehouse, asking for IDs. What kind of mess are you guys tangled up in? We don't want any trouble."

Fergus raised a hand, attempting to calm Rodney. "Relax, mate. No one's in any danger. It was just an incident involving a crooked cop. I'll explain everything later."

Rodney looked skeptical. "You're kidding, right?"

"I kid you not," Fergus replied with a tired grin. "How about this, I'll tell you the whole story tonight over a barbecue. Stop by the butcher on your way back, grab some steaks, and don't forget to hit the bottle shop. Bring everyone along. It'll be a good feed, and I'll give you the big picture."

Once back at the camp, Fergus set to work preparing for the evening. He dragged out the brand-new Weber BBQ, arranged tables and chairs from the lunchroom donga in front of the amenities building, and switched on the floodlights, which bathed the area in bright, clean light. He sliced up two whole rumps he'd bought earlier that morning and put a large stainless steel boiler on the stove to bring the chat potatoes to a boil.

Just as Fergus and Wes were setting up the BBQ, Tim rolled into camp behind the wheel of the twin-steer Kenworth truck. He climbed down, stretched, and accepted a cold stubbie of beer from Wes with a grin.

"Looks like my timing's perfect," Tim said, cracking open the bottle.

"Spot on," Fergus replied. "The crew from the Gatehouse is coming over. They were pretty shaken up by last night's commotion, so I figured I'd put on a feed, hand out some beers, and clear things up."

By the time Rodney, Belinda, Jason, and Allison arrived, carrying eskies loaded with drinks, the sun had dipped below the horizon, and the floodlights illuminated the camp like a football field. They walked the 400 meters from the Gatehouse, chatting quietly among themselves as they approached. Fergus greeted them warmly and introduced everyone to Wes and Tim.

Once they were all seated in the makeshift dining area, Fergus raised a hand to get their attention. "Alright, before I have too many more beers, let me tell you what happened last night. You deserve to know."

He began his story from the very beginning, recounting the accident that had claimed Amelia's life, Kirkland's persistent harassment afterward, and the tense events of the previous night. He was careful to stay within the limits of the confidentiality agreement they had signed but still managed to convey enough of the story for everyone to understand the gravity of the situation.

By the time he finished, there was a heavy silence around the table. Belinda shook her head in disbelief. "So, you're telling us that after all that, we won't see a word about it in the news?"

"Exactly," Fergus confirmed. "The whole thing's being kept under wraps. As far as the police are concerned, it's hush-hush. They don't want any bad publicity, especially not for one of their own."

Jason exhaled slowly, shaking his head. "Mate, that's a hell of a story. Can't say I envy you, dealing with that nut-job Kirkland."

Wes chuckled softly. "If he comes back, I'll be happy to deal with him again."

Everyone laughed, though there was an underlying tension that didn't go unnoticed. Despite the jovial atmosphere, they all knew that things might not be over. But for now, they had food, drinks, and good company, and that was enough.

Rodney raised his beer in a toast. "To Fergus, Wes, and Tim, may the next few weeks be a lot less eventful."

The group laughed, clinking their bottles together, and the evening carried on in good spirits. But even as they enjoyed their meal under the bright floodlights, Fergus couldn't help but glance toward the dark edges of the camp, wondering when the next storm would come.

Everyone was visibly moved by Fergus's story, and the girls, Belinda and Allison, couldn't help but express sympathy for Mitch. "Poor Mitch," they said. "He must carry a huge hatred for the police, and probably for the Aboriginals too, considering they were responsible for Fergus being sent to prison."

Fergus gave a small, weary nod. "It hasn't exactly helped my feelings toward the police either. And as for the Aboriginals, well, it's complicated. But having Kirkland constantly pursuing me has made things even worse."

He hadn't been given any clear indication about what would become of Kirkland, but he felt confident the disgraced officer wouldn't be stationed in Cooktown any longer. Regardless, Fergus and Wes planned to visit the police station the next morning to reclaim the rifles that had been seized during the dramatic events of the previous night.

Despite the tense backstory, the evening turned into a lively and enjoyable gathering. The laughter and camaraderie around the barbecue helped ease the tension lingering from the previous night. The last to leave was Rodney, who finally headed home around one o'clock in the morning. By that time, Fergus was utterly shattered, having been awake for almost twenty-four hours straight. Tim had retired at about ten, while Wes had called it a night around eleven-thirty. Once Rodney left, Fergus didn't waste another second, he headed straight to his donga and didn't emerge until nearly eleven the next morning.

By the time Fergus finally surfaced, Tim was already up and working on some minor repairs to the Kenworth twin-steer truck. Fergus strolled over, blinking against the late morning sun, and looked over the truck with a critical eye. After a few minutes of inspecting the unit, he gave an approving nod. "Looks good, Tim. I'm impressed. Now that we've got the gear sorted, we need to start thinking about finding operators."

Tim wiped his hands on a rag and leaned against the truck, grinning. "Funny you should mention that. I was chatting with Jason at the barbecue last night. He told me he used to operate an excavator like ours down in Brisbane. He's got his ticket for it, so he's certified. Plus, he knows a guy, the former council road manager in Cooktown. Apparently, he's a damn good operator, just got sacked for drinking on the job. He's part Aboriginal but a solid bloke, according to Jason."

Fergus raised an eyebrow, considering this new information. "A former council road manager, huh? Might be worth looking into, as long as we're clear about the no-drinking rule. We don't need any more problems."

Tim nodded in agreement. "Yeah, Jason seemed to think he'd be reliable if he stayed off the grog. Could be worth a chat."

Fergus mulled it over, his mind already working through the logistics. They had the equipment, and now, if they could assemble a decent team, they'd be ready to start serious work. "Alright, let's get through today. Once we sort out the rifles at the police station, we'll go talk to Jason and see if we can meet this operator. If he's any good, we might have our first hire."

Tim grinned. "Sounds like a plan."

With that, Fergus felt a renewed sense of purpose. After the chaos of the past few days, it was time to focus on building something productive. Kirkland and the past might still be lurking in the background, but for now, they had a business to run, and that was something Fergus could control.

"What do you reckon, Tim? Let's give Jason a job. First thing he can do is track down that former council worker and bring him out here for a yarn," Fergus suggested.

"I was thinking the exact same thing, Fergus," Tim replied, nodding in agreement.

Meanwhile, Wes was in the mess donga enjoying a late breakfast when Fergus found him. "Hey, don't forget we're heading into Cooktown to the police station to pick up our rifles. Make sure you've got your firearms license and any rifle permits with you."

Wes looked up from his plate and gave a confident nod. "No worries. I've got everything in order."

The New March

A short while later, they pulled up outside the modest Cooktown police station. As they stepped inside, a young constable greeted them with a polite, "Good morning."

"Morning," Fergus responded. "I'm Fergus Laird, and this is Werner Fischer. We're here to collect our firearms that were seized from my property near Shiptons Flat the night before last."

The constable's casual demeanour stiffened, and he sat up straighter in his chair. "Ah... yes, I see. Just a moment, I'll call Senior Sergeant Sutton." He disappeared into the back room, and they could hear him relaying a message over the radio.

Returning moments later, the constable offered an apologetic smile. "Sergeant Sutton will be with you shortly. Sorry for the wait."

"No problem," Fergus assured him, though he couldn't help but notice the constable sneaking a few curious glances in Wes's direction. Wes, as usual, remained calm and impassive.

After a brief wait, the front door opened, and Senior Sergeant Sutton walked in, clearly looking as though he'd been disturbed from some well-earned rest. His expression was a mix of irritation and fatigue as he glanced in their direction.

"Do you have your permits and licenses with you?" he asked without preamble.

Both men stood and approached the counter, placing their documents in front of him. The sergeant picked up Wes's papers first, reading them aloud in a slow, deliberate tone.

"Mannlicher-Schoenauer M72 .22-250 Remington, serial number ZCX567GF998, and Mannlicher-Schoenauer M72 S/T Model .375 H&H Magnum, serial number CBX554WS87V... wait here while I retrieve your rifles."

The sergeant disappeared into the back and returned shortly, carrying two rifle cases. He opened each one, carefully checked the serial numbers, and handed the rifles over to Wes. "Sign here," he instructed, sliding a clipboard across the counter.

After Wes had signed, the sergeant gave him a sideways glance. "What are you using a .375 caliber for? That's serious firepower."

Wes smiled faintly. "I used it for shooting camels in Western Australia. And I hear it's also very good for hunting pigs." His grin widened, but the sergeant didn't share the humour and merely grunted in response.

Turning to Fergus, the sergeant picked up his permits and read them aloud in the same deliberate manner. "Winchester Model 94 Carbine, serial number 7709HQ1, and Winchester Model 94, serial number 7762298ZA... wait here."

He returned moments later with the two Winchester rifles. Unlike Wes, Fergus didn't have cases for his rifles, so the sergeant inspected the firearms directly. Eyeing the shorter rifle suspiciously, he frowned.

"Why is this one cut down?" he asked, clearly skeptical.

Fergus sighed internally but kept his voice steady. "It's not cut down. One's a rifle, the other's a carbine, about four inches shorter by design."

The sergeant leaned in, scrutinising the carbine's barrel as though searching for evidence of tampering. "Why do you need a long one and a short one?"

Fergus shrugged. "The carbine's for my son. When I bought it, he was nine, and my rifle was too big for him to handle."

As soon as the words left his mouth, Fergus regretted them. The sergeant's expression hardened. "The rifles are registered in your name. Nobody else is legally allowed to use them, and there's an age limit for firearm use. You should know better."

Fergus clenched his jaw, suppressing his irritation. "Whatever," he muttered, signing the paperwork. He picked up his rifles and turned to leave.

Just as they reached the door, the sergeant's voice called after them, laced with sarcasm. "I'll be watching you closely. And just so you know, nobody's ever going to take my gun from me."

Fergus paused but didn't bother to turn around. Wes, however, glanced back briefly, his expression unreadable. "Let's hope we don't have to find out, yar," Wes said with a knowing grin, the kind of smile that was both a little devious and entirely confident. It was a smile not unlike the one Fergus had seen in old photographs of surrendered German officers, proud in defeat, commanding respect yet subtly unsettling. It was the type of smile that seemed to suggest superiority, leaving the onlooker with a sense of inferiority.

Fergus caught the glint in Wes's eyes and couldn't help but chuckle. The sergeant, however, wasn't laughing. He had recognised the expression on Wes's face all too well. His gaze faltered, and he quickly looked away, unable to hold Wes's steady, unyielding stare. It was as if the sergeant's pride had been momentarily undermined, and he couldn't maintain the mask of authority.

The two men exited the station, their footsteps echoing softly in the otherwise quiet street. As they passed through the door, they could hear the muffled sound of the sergeant's voice, growing louder by the second.

"Don't ever disturb me for something like this again!" the sergeant barked at the constable, his frustration evident. "This could have been handled easily without dragging me out of bed."

"But, sir, you told me explicitly to call you when Mr. Laird arrived to collect his firearms," the constable replied, his tone cautious.

The sergeant's response was immediate and thunderous. "Don't fucking argue with me, Sonny Jim!" His voice rang out across the small station and, to Fergus and Wes's amusement, it could be heard clearly all the way down Charlotte Street.

The sound of the sergeant's outburst hung in the air for a moment, but neither Fergus nor Wes commented on it. They were both content, walking away from the station with their rifles in hand and a shared understanding that the tension from the encounter was nothing more than a passing irritation. The sergeant's anger was his problem, not theirs.

As they continued down the street, Wes shot Fergus a sideways glance. "That was fun," he said, his grin still in place, though it was now a little more knowing. "Let's hope we don't see him again anytime soon."

Fergus chuckled, his gaze shifting to the horizon. "If we do, we'll just have to hope he remembers his manners."

"You know, Fergus," Wes said, his tone oddly serious, "we could dig a big pit at Stezland, big enough for that fat copper and his car, and he could be a missing cop that nobody misses at all... and would never be found. What do you think?"

Wes's words hung in the air as he continued, "I'm thinking that this one will also make trouble for us."

Fergus raised an eyebrow, momentarily startled by the suggestion, but then a grin tugged at the corners of his mouth. Wes was half-joking, yet the underlying seriousness in his voice suggested there was more truth to his words than humour. Fergus didn't reply immediately; instead, he started to think, really think, about what Wes had said. As absurd as it sounded, with a bit of planning, it wouldn't be that difficult to make someone disappear. He wasn't sure if it was the idea itself or Wes's calm delivery of it, but the more he thought about it, the easier it seemed.

For the time being, though, he opted for silence. It wasn't the first time he'd heard a dark idea come out of Wes's mouth. The man was efficient, coldly pragmatic when it came to getting things done, and Fergus had learned to appreciate that, even when it came with a touch of menace.

At Stezland, excavation work had begun for the power lines to be laid beneath the road. The road construction soon followed, and once the road reached the other side of the gorge, it opened the floodgates for construction materials to be delivered, allowing the builder to start work on the house.

However, road construction at Stezland came to an abrupt halt when the urgency of the project had passed. The builder no longer needed power for the time being, as they were relying on generators. The track through the gorge, while not ideal, was passable enough when dry for the workers' vehicles and medium-sized delivery trucks to access the site.

In the meantime, Tim had secured a sizeable civil project from the Cooktown Shire. They were tasked with replacing a washed-out bridge and rebuilding a three-kilometre stretch of road. Fergus was pleased with this turn of events, as his bank balance had taken a hit due to his recent capital purchases for equipment. This job, while large, would give him some financial breathing room.

The project, however, came with a few challenges. To carry out the work properly, they would need additional equipment, including another compactor and roller, along with a more advanced grader. Tim had included the costs for these items in the price he'd submitted to the council. The proposal came in at over twelve million dollars, an extortionate sum for a job that, quite frankly, they didn't need. But to their surprise, the council had responded swiftly, asking, "How soon can you get started?" They explained that the Aboriginal settlement of Hopevale could be cut off during the wet season, which would create a major headache, particularly with Federal Parliament. That alone was enough to push the council into action.

Fergus couldn't help but chuckle. "Tim, you're a bloody genius," he muttered under his breath, impressed at how easily the council had been swayed.

They didn't really need the job, but the council seemed desperate. And that desperation had a price. With the deal in place, Fergus had more breathing room, but a lingering feeling told him that the higher stakes would only come with more complications down the road. Still, he wasn't complaining. For now, things were looking up. But he knew better than to count his chickens before they hatched, especially in a place like Stezland.

Tim had made strategic moves from the outset. He engaged workers from Hopevale and took it a step further by training some of them to become skilled machine operators. In addition, he organised transportation for the workers, using two buses to ferry them from Hopevale to the work sites. This not only provided a vital service to the workers but also helped safeguard their equipment, which had to be left on-site overnight. The added security was a bonus, and it seemed that the local Hopevale people knew better than to jeopardise their own livelihoods by targeting the project. This cultural understanding proved invaluable, as it ensured that the equipment remained safe, and the project was completed within the designated contract period. The job's success didn't stop there. The team managed to finish ahead of schedule, earning a substantial bonus, which Fergus promptly distributed among the settlement people. It was a gesture that reinforced the bond between the workers and the project, fostering goodwill and trust.

As the work progressed, it became clear why the previous civil contractors had abandoned the job: the high costs associated with replacing and repairing damaged or missing equipment, as well as the loss of over thirty thousand litres of diesel fuel and oils, had drained their resources. This was a major setback for the earlier contractors, but for Tim and his team, it was a lesson in preparation and care. Tim's logistical planning and community engagement had set the project on a far more stable footing.

Once the project was completed, and with the bonus distributed, Tim's success opened the door for more work. The Cooktown Shire offered them another project, this time on the Rossville to Bloomfield road. The scope of the work was significant, and as before, workers were recruited from the settlements at both Bloomfield and Wujil Wujil. The familiarity of the workers with the terrain and local conditions made them the ideal choice for the job.

With Tim handling the earthmoving and machinery side of things, Fergus could step back and focus on other aspects of the operation. Tim had proven he was more than capable of running the heavy machinery and organizing the work with minimal input from Fergus. This allowed Fergus and Wes more time to focus on the long-term plans for Stezland, particularly the cattle muster.

No one had any real idea of how many cattle were on Stezland, and that posed a significant challenge. The land was vast, and the task of rounding up the cattle would require careful planning, equipment, and manpower. It wasn't just a logistical task, it was a test of their ability to organise a large-scale operation in a remote and often unforgiving environment.

Colin Freebody had shared some valuable insight with Fergus about the cattle yards on Stezland. He explained that there were three sets of yards scattered across the property, though they hadn't been in use for some twenty years. When Colin last worked with them, the yards were in poor condition. However, they were built with durable hardwood, which might still make them serviceable for certain tasks. He sketched a rough map showing the locations of these yards and clarified that, while they were not ideal for the entire cattle processing operation, they could still serve a purpose for draughting, marking, ear tagging, or dehorning.

However, there were significant limitations. The yards lacked scales and loading ramps, which made it impossible to properly transport cattle, particularly since the roads around the area were not suitable for heavy transport vehicles. Once the cattle were mustered and worked in the smaller yards, the bullocks were traditionally driven down to the larger yards that used to be situated halfway between the 'Gatehouse' and an unnamed creek. Unfortunately, those yards had been destroyed in a bushfire years ago, a disaster that not only wiped out the cattle yards but also knocked out the power lines for Murray's new house.

Despite the setbacks, Colin was still confident that a system could be designed to work efficiently on Stezland. He mentioned a system he had seen during a trip to Western Australia about seven years ago. According to Colin, this method could be easily adapted for Stezland's unique conditions, potentially solving many of the issues that had plagued the cattle operations in the past.

Fergus, always looking for practical solutions, agreed to pay Colin for his time and expertise in designing a new system that would improve the cattle operations on the property. The old man's experience was something Fergus valued, and he was willing to invest in making the necessary changes to make Stezland more efficient and productive.

"You've got the equipment to make it possible," Colin said, looking at Fergus with a knowing glance. What he meant was that Fergus had the resources to repair or construct the necessary roads and culverts, which would be key to transporting the cattle more effectively. But it would require some investment.

"If you're prepared to invest some of your own resources into this, then it will work," Colin continued, his tone confident. "It'll make it easier to get the cattle down to the main yards, the ones you really need to use. Before, when we were droving them, we had a whole bunch of cattle down here that we didn't want. They'd keep sneaking into the herd, and we couldn't separate them properly. There were generally only four of us handling the droving, and we just didn't have the feed for all the cattle once we got them down to the big yards."

Colin paused for a moment, making sure Fergus understood the challenge they'd faced.

"But by transporting them down, you only bring the ones you want, those you've already selected. You can manage the numbers much more easily, and you won't waste resources feeding cattle that don't need to be there."

Fergus nodded, appreciating Colin's insight. The old man had lived through the challenges of running cattle on Stezland and had a clear understanding of what would make the process more efficient. The idea of transporting cattle, instead of driving them, sounded like a simple yet effective solution. It would require upgrading the roads, building new infrastructure, and making significant investments in the right equipment, but the potential benefits were enormous. With the right system in place, Stezland could streamline its cattle operations and reduce costs, all while improving the handling and management of their herd. It was a plan that made sense, and Fergus was more than willing to see it through.

The Muster

Colin's vision for improving the cattle yards and making the muster process more efficient at Stezland was both practical and forward-thinking. His plan began with building a new set of cattle yards near the 'Gatehouse,' strategically located where there was a reliable water supply from the unnamed creek. These new yards would be constructed from steel for durability, and would include a loading ramp, an essential addition to facilitate the smooth handling of cattle. The existing yards, while serviceable, would need some modifications. Colin's idea was to transform them into 'self-mustering' yards, which would also be built from steel, ensuring a uniform, low-maintenance infrastructure for years to come. Any future repairs would also be made with steel components, creating a strong, lasting foundation for the operation.

Next, Colin proposed the creation of a mobile loading ramp that would revolutionize how cattle were handled at Stezland. This ramp would be equipped with locks, draughting gates, and a set of scales, all integrated into a seamless, mobile system. The design of the ramp itself was innovative: it would be constructed with a turret for a prime mover fitted just beneath the top of the ramp. This would be similar to the coupling on a semi-trailer, but instead of cargo decking, it would feature cattle loading rails. This clever design would ensure the correct loading height, aligning perfectly with the height of stock transport loading doors, taking into account both the turret and the thickness of the decking.

The mobile loading ramp would be built to exacting specifications. The deck would be two meters in length, followed by a three-meter ramp that would slope down before leveling off into a nine-meter race for the crush, locks, draughting gates, and scales. In total, the ramp would span fourteen meters in length. To make the ramp mobile, it would be fitted with dual detachable wheels positioned about three-quarters of the way along its length. These wheels could be removed easily using high-lift jacks, ensuring the ramp could be repositioned quickly and efficiently.

The real genius of the design lay in its mobility. The ramp could be easily moved by a prime mover, which would also allow it to be attached to whichever cattle yard was in use at any given time. Once the ramp was set into its designated location at the yard, the prime mover could be detached and used for other trailers, making the entire process even more versatile. The flexibility and efficiency of the system would be a game-changer for the operation, allowing the team to manage cattle in a way that was quicker and less labor-intensive.

Colin's drawing of the design was clear and detailed, a scale blueprint that made his vision come to life. Fergus, seeing the practicality and ingenuity of the plan, handed the drawing over to Tim, instructing him to have it fabricated in the new workshops that were being built at the camp. With Tim's expertise and the resources available at the camp, the fabrication of this mobile loading ramp would soon be underway, marking a major step toward modernizing the cattle operations at Stezland and setting a new standard for efficiency in the industry.

It had been two years since Fergus had first set foot on Stezland, and in that time, he had made significant progress, transforming the property into something that was beginning to reflect his hard work and vision. Yet, despite the milestones he had reached, there was still so much left to do. The landscape of Stezland was changing, but it was clear that the journey was far from over.

Mitchell, now seventeen, had spent the Christmas school holidays at the camp, a welcome presence in the midst of all the work. Fergus had bought him an HZJ Land Cruiser for his birthday, a gesture that spoke volumes about how much he valued his son's presence and involvement in the family business. However, there were conditions attached to the gift, Fergus had restricted Mitchell to using the vehicle only around the property until he turned eighteen. It was a way to give him a taste of freedom while still ensuring that he respected the responsibilities that came with owning such a vehicle. Fergus couldn't help but feel a sense of pride as he watched his son take on more responsibility around the camp, but he also knew that Mitchell was growing up quickly and would soon be ready to take on even more.

The house, which had once seemed like a distant dream, was now all but complete. The power had been connected, and the place had begun to feel like home. It was no longer just a construction site but a living, breathing space where Fergus could finally put his feet up at the end of the day. The transformation was a testament to the countless hours of hard work and planning, but it still needed a final layer of polish to truly feel like a home.

To help manage the day-to-day needs of the property, Fergus had employed a Vietnamese couple to serve as the cook, housekeeper, maid, and gardener. They had moved into a small unit at the back of the house, helping to keep things running smoothly. The couple was a quiet, efficient presence, taking care of the chores that would otherwise take up too much of Fergus's time. Their arrival had made life at Stezland a little easier, allowing Fergus to focus on the larger goals while knowing that the small details were being taken care of.

As Fergus stood in the doorway of the house one evening, watching the sun dip behind the hills, he reflected on how much had changed in just two short years. The sense of accomplishment was there, but so was the understanding that the work was never truly done. There would always be something else to fix, build, or improve, but that was the nature of life at Stezland, an ever-evolving project, one step at a time.

The three old cattle yards had undergone extensive repairs and modifications, transforming them into efficient "self mustering" yards. The process involved not just fixing structural issues but also making significant upgrades to ensure the yards could operate seamlessly. First, bores for water had been established or reinstated, ensuring a reliable water supply for the cattle. Alongside these, water troughs were installed, along with hay handlers to manage the feeding process more efficiently.

One of the key features of the new system was the addition of 'one-way' gates. These gates, only one meter wide, were equipped with heavy springs on the hinge side, allowing the gate to close automatically across the fixed post. This design ensured that only one animal could enter at a time, preventing any cattle from slipping out once inside the yard. The one-way system was critical for maintaining order within the yards and reducing stress on the animals during mustering.

Alongside these modifications, the yards had to be adjusted to accommodate the newly completed mobile loading contraption, which would become known as the 'Freebody.' This innovative system, a long-awaited addition to the operation, was now finished and ready for its first test. The loading ramp was a marvel of engineering, designed for ease of use and maximum efficiency, making it a game changer for handling cattle in the future.

Meanwhile, new all-steel cattle yards had been constructed near the camp and the 'Gatehouse'. These yards featured two loading ramps and three large holding yards designed to accommodate up to six hundred head of cattle. Four water troughs were strategically placed and fed from both the unnamed creek and two newly drilled bores, ensuring an ample water supply for the cattle, even during the hottest months.

Fergus had put significant pressure on Tim to finish the roads leading to the cattle yards before the wet season arrived, as they needed to be ready for mustering between June and November. The looming deadline meant that additional resources were required to expedite the process. To meet this demand, they purchased a fourth grader, this time a massive Komatsu model with a 426 HP engine. This new grader was the largest they had acquired yet, specifically for use on council road rebuilds. The purchase allowed them to retire the old Cat grader they had initially bought for Stezland, turning it into a dedicated station grader. To operate this new equipment, a skilled man from Wujil Wujil was trained, adding another valuable worker to the team and ensuring that the roads could be kept in top condition year-round.

The expansion and upgrades at Stezland were becoming a well-oiled machine, but the scale of the operations was beginning to test the limits of what they could accomplish. Still, with each new addition, Fergus saw the potential for more efficiency and productivity, pushing the boundaries of what the property could achieve. The upcoming mustering season would be a crucial test of all the improvements, and Fergus was determined to ensure everything was in place for a smooth and successful operation.

The camp had undergone significant expansion, now housing a total of ten accommodation dongas, providing ample space for the growing workforce. Each of these dongas was equipped with the basic comforts needed for long stays, ensuring that workers had a reliable place to rest after a hard day's work. In addition to the accommodation, another double office donga had been added to accommodate the administrative needs of the team. This new office space was designed to handle the increasing volume of paperwork and planning required for the various projects at Stezland, from road construction to cattle management.

The mess and kitchen donga had also been expanded, reflecting the growing number of people working at the camp. The larger kitchen was now fully equipped with commercial-grade appliances, ensuring meals could be prepared quickly and efficiently for the workforce. A spacious dining area was added to accommodate everyone at once, fostering a sense of camaraderie among the workers during meal times. The upgraded facilities ensured that the camp ran smoothly, even as it accommodated more personnel.

An additional amenities donga had also been built to meet the increased demand for bathroom and shower facilities. This new donga, strategically placed to be easily accessible from the accommodation and work areas, helped reduce congestion during the morning and evening rush, ensuring everyone had access to the necessary facilities at any time.

Fergus had made it clear that he intended to keep his office at the camp, as it allowed him to stay closely involved with all aspects of the operation. His office remained the heart of the decision-making process, a place where he could handle the important business matters that kept the project moving forward. The new offices were designated for Tim and Wes, allowing them their own space to manage their respective tasks more efficiently. Tim's office, with its proximity to the earthmoving and construction operations, was ideal for overseeing the machinery and roadwork. Wes's office, on the other hand, was situated close to the livestock and cattle management areas, giving him the necessary oversight for the stock-related projects.

The new setup allowed for a smoother flow of communication and made it easier for everyone to focus on their specific roles while maintaining a strong sense of teamwork. With the camp's infrastructure expanding to accommodate the growing needs of Stezland, it was becoming a hub of activity, with each new addition designed to ensure efficiency and productivity.

The New March

The first official cattle muster on Stezland in nearly..., no one seemed to know exactly, took place that year, marking a significant milestone for the property. Though unofficial musters had occurred every couple of years, according to local gossip, this was the first formal attempt in decades. It was a momentous event, one that brought both anticipation and excitement, as the property's infrastructure had finally reached a level that made such a muster not only possible but efficient.

The most notable change was the modification of the cattle yards into 'self-mustering' facilities, a system designed to simplify the process and reduce the need for regular human intervention. With the yards equipped for self-mustering, cattle could freely seek water and food in the months leading up to the wet season when natural resources began to dwindle. The holding yard gates would be closed but left unlocked, allowing cattle to find their way into the holding yards through one-way entry gates. This design ensured that the cattle could enter but not exit, keeping them contained without the need for constant human supervision. Water troughs were turned on, and hay handlers were regularly filled, ensuring the cattle had access to sufficient feed and water as they congregated in the yards. Over time, the yards would hold all the cattle from the surrounding area, streamlining the mustering process.

For this inaugural muster, Fergus had decided to contract a team based at Cow Bay, a location just over 100 kilometres from Shiptons Flat. The muster was to begin on Stezland's eastern boundary, which was approximately 30 kilometres from Cow Bay. The contractor, experienced and well-acquainted with the land, quoted $30 per head for the cattle

The New March

to be mustered, marked, tagged, draughted, and loaded. Fergus observed that the contractor seemed to have an extensive knowledge of the terrain, which instilled confidence in him.

The 'Freebody' loading ramp was set up at the first, or highest, set of yards, ready for the incoming cattle. The first muster brought in 104 mixed-head cattle, with 20 calves to be marked, tagged, and released. There were two bulls to be tagged and let go, along with 30 cows and heifers, at least 11 of which were in calf. The remaining 52 were bullocks, which were designated for transportation to the camp yards. As Fergus coordinated the transport, the second muster began at the number two yards, bringing in 130 head, one bull, 18 calves, 37 cows, and 74 bullocks for transport. The final muster, at the number three yards, resulted in 110 head, including five bulls, 12 calves, 28 cows, and 65 bullocks for the camp yards.

Once all the bullocks had been placed in the camp yards, neighboring properties were contacted to inspect the herd for any cattle that might belong to them, based on their brand. Those cattle were returned to their respective owners for a fee of $50 per head. After the cattle were accounted for and the muster was complete, Fergus was left with 191 bullocks, which were transported to the cattle market in Charters Towers. The sale of these bullocks brought in a total of $171,900, with an average price of $900 per head. However, after deducting mustering costs of $10,320, transport costs from yards to yards of $9,000, and the $19,100 cost for transporting the cattle to Charters Towers ($100 per head for the 800km trip), Fergus was left with $133,000 in net profit.

Despite the seemingly profitable outcome, Fergus knew the process still wasn't as efficient as it could be. He had to pay his own labor costs, and some of the revenue had to be allocated toward the cost of the yards. However, he was optimistic about the future. "Next year will be much better," he thought to himself. Without the need to contract out for mustering, he would save on those expenses, and by investing in his own cattle truck for transportation between yards, he could cut an additional $20,000 from his costs each year. That savings could be redirected into hiring someone with expertise in cattle management, something Fergus had learned he was sorely lacking. When it came to cattle, he realised, he knew very little.

Restructuring

Fergus had started to notice a troubling pattern: while there seemed to be plenty of money coming in, it felt as though an equal, if not greater, amount was flowing out. He was unsure if he was making or losing money, and that uncertainty gnawed at him. He knew this was a dangerous position to be in, but finding an accountant in Cooktown was nearly impossible. That was until one evening, when he ran into a man he thought he recognised.

It was at the RSL club, where Fergus saw a man working behind the bar, a face that lingered in his memory. After some time, he placed it: the man had once been involved in commercial construction accounting in Brisbane. Fergus couldn't shake the feeling that he knew him from somewhere, so he took a chance and approached him.

The man, whose name was Ken Miller, was initially hesitant. He was quick to make it clear that his past was behind him, and Cooktown was where he'd chosen to live because no one there would recognise him. Fergus didn't quite understand, but Ken's words were enough to pique his curiosity. "Well, that was a fucking mistake, by the looks of it," Ken muttered, a sense of resignation in his voice.

Ken revealed that he had served a ten-year prison sentence for fraud, a conviction that had ultimately ended his career in Brisbane's construction industry. Despite the dark past, Ken insisted he hadn't officially studied accountancy nor was he a registered accountant, but he was confident in his ability to manage numbers. "I know my sums," he'd said with a half-grin.

Fergus saw an opportunity. "Would you be interested in a business proposition?" he asked.

Ken's response was swift and blunt. "No fucking way, my friend. No fucking way am I going back to jail." He shook his head vehemently. "This is a shit job behind the bar, but at least it's honest money. I don't have to look over my back."

Fergus was undeterred. "I meant something legit. Everything I do is perfectly legal. I just need help with bookkeeping, that's all. I need an accountant, nothing more, let me tell you."

After some more back-and-forth, Fergus managed to convince Ken to meet him the next morning. He offered to take him to Stezland, give him a tour of the operation, and let him think it over. Ken agreed, albeit cautiously.

The next day, around 9:30 AM, they set off for Stezland. On the way, Fergus showed Ken the impressive progress on the property: the new cattle yards, the 'Gatehouse,' and the camp, which was now beginning to look like a small town with its fifteen buildings, workshop, and machinery storage compound. Fergus pointed towards the horizon, "My house is down that way. Eight kilometres from here. I'm finally moving in next week."

Ken listened with growing interest but admitted that he was still renting a "shitbox" one-bedroom flat in a rundown building in Cooktown. He was actively looking for somewhere else to live, though he knew accommodation options were scarce. Fergus, ever the generous host, offered, "You're welcome to have my donga when I move in next week. It'll save you the trouble of commuting, too. I know you don't have a car."

When they arrived at Fergus's office, he gave Ken a more detailed picture of what he had inherited and the work he had begun to put in place. He explained that he needed someone who could set up and maintain an accounting system that could track his business operations, which were diverse and growing by the day.

Ken seemed more intrigued now that he had seen the scale of the operation firsthand. He began to ask more probing questions, showing a keen interest in the logistics of the business. "Is this a full-time position?" he asked. "What sort of dollars are you thinking of paying? I think I can easily do what you need. I can even set up a structure that would split the different activities into separate companies under a major head office."

Fergus could sense the wheels turning in Ken's mind, and he was hopeful that this could be the beginning of a solution to his growing financial concerns. The man had no formal credentials, but his practical experience and sharp understanding of business structures might be just what Fergus needed. This wasn't just about keeping the books balanced, it was about creating a solid foundation for a growing empire. And it seemed that Ken Miller, despite his past, might be the right person to help him build it.

Fergus and Ken quickly came to an agreement on a salary, and as part of the arrangement, Ken would move out to the camp and take over Fergus's donga when he vacated it the following week. In addition, Fergus promised to organise a company car for Ken's exclusive use, though in the interim,

Ken could use Fergus's Land Rover to get around. It seemed like a mutually beneficial situation. Ken was eager to get started, particularly with designing a structure for Stezland's expanding operations. Fergus, for his part, felt a sense of relief knowing that he now had someone capable to help navigate the complex financial aspects of his growing business.

After finalising the details, Fergus took Ken back to Cooktown and dropped him off at the RSL club where he worked behind the bar. As he did so, Fergus noticed a police car cruising by at a crawl, with Police Senior Sergeant Sutton driving. The sergeant's eyes lingered on both Fergus and Ken, and Fergus couldn't shake the feeling that something was off. His instincts told him that Sutton's slow drive by wasn't just a coincidence.

Back at the office, Fergus decided to follow up on his suspicions. He called his solicitor, Brian Haptu, but Brian was on another call. His secretary assured Fergus that Brian would return his call shortly. While waiting, Fergus decided to make use of the office's new cappuccino machine, which Wes had arranged, and brewed himself a coffee. Just as he was settling back into his chair, the phone rang, Brian was on the line.

They exchanged pleasantries, and after catching up on a few things, Fergus mentioned his concerns regarding consorting laws. He explained that he had recently hired Ken Miller as his accountant, outlining Ken's criminal past and giving Brian a rundown of the police sergeant's interest in Ken earlier that morning.

Brian listened carefully before assuring Fergus that he would look into Ken's full prison term and any possible obligations or liabilities that might still be hanging over him. Consorting, as Brian explained, typically applied to situations where there were at least three people involved, so as long as Ken wasn't still under any legal obligations, there shouldn't be an issue.

Within thirty minutes, Brian called back with good news. Ken had been fully discharged and there were no remaining obligations. There were no legal constraints on him, and as long as Ken stayed clear of any further trouble, he was free to operate without issue.

Fergus, though relieved, couldn't let go of the nagging feeling about Senior Sergeant Sutton's apparent scrutiny. He mentioned this to Brian, noting how the sergeant had been hassling them over minor truck-related traffic infringements recently. Fergus wanted to ensure that everything was above board and that there was nothing lurking in the background that could come back to haunt him.

Brian reassured him that as far as the law was concerned, there were no red flags with Ken Miller. With that, Fergus could breathe easier, but the unease about Sutton's behaviour lingered in the back of his mind. He knew it wasn't just about traffic tickets, it seemed personal. But for now, it looked like he had the legal green light to move forward with Ken, and that was a weight off his shoulders.

After just two weeks of observing and analysing the operation at Stezland, Ken Miller had come up with a comprehensive proposal that would restructure the entire setup. He presented it to Fergus with a level of clarity and confidence that immediately caught Fergus's attention. The plan outlined a structure that would allow Stezland's various ventures to operate under a unified yet tax-efficient framework.

Ken's proposal was simple yet highly effective. He suggested that the principal company be named Stezland Proprietary Limited (P/L), which would own the land known as Stezland, with one significant exception: Fergus's private subdivision of 250 acres, where his home was situated, would be under his personal ownership. This structure would also encompass all equipment used by the sub-companies under the Stezland umbrella. Stezland P/L would act as the administrator of all the sub-companies, streamlining management and operations.

Ken proposed the following subsidiary companies under the Stezland umbrella:

Stezland Civil Engineers and Earthmoving Contractors Proprietary Limited (P/L): This company would lease the camp, workshops, compounds, and all equipment from Stezland P/L.

Stezland Pastoral Proprietary Limited (P/L): This company would lease the grazing pastures, cattle yards, and water facilities from Stezland P/L.

Stezland Raw Materials Proprietary Limited (P/L): This entity would lease the quarry from Stezland P/L.

Stezland Transport Proprietary Limited (P/L): This company would lease prime movers and trailers and rent premises from Stezland P/L.

Ken explained that by structuring the business in this way, significant savings could be realised, particularly by avoiding unnecessary taxation on well-earned revenue. Capital investments could also be written off, further reducing the financial burden on the operation.

To give Fergus a clearer idea of how this structure would benefit the business, Ken offered a practical example. He explained that if Stezland Earthmoving Contractors earned one million dollars annually, the company's outgoings, staff wages, materials from Stezland Raw Materials, and the lease of equipment from Stezland P/L, totalled $950,000. This would leave a taxable income of $50,000. At a 30% tax rate, the tax bill would amount to just $15,000, a significantly reduced tax liability compared to the million-dollar turnover.

Ken outlined that similar situations would apply across the various Stezland companies. By minimising taxable income in each company, including the principal Stezland P/L, the overall tax burden could be drastically reduced to only about 5% of the turnover for each company.

After carefully reviewing Ken's proposal, Fergus felt that it was an exceptional plan that would bring substantial financial benefits to Stezland. However, he knew it was crucial to ensure that the system was legally sound. With that in mind, he sent the proposal to his solicitor, Brian Haptu, via facsimile, asking for his legal opinion.

Brian, in turn, forwarded the document to a taxation specialist chartered accountant for further review. The accountant's response was highly favourable. He confirmed that the proposed structure was a brilliant approach, although it was pushing the boundaries of what the Australian Taxation Office (ATO) might consider typical. However, he reassured Fergus that the system, as designed, was fully within the laws and regulations of the ATO. It was a strategy that operated "under the radar" but still adhered to the legal framework.

Brian forwarded the accountant's findings to Fergus, who, after receiving the legal confirmation, wasted no time in setting the plan into motion. He instructed Brian to begin the process of registering all the Stezland companies, ensuring that the operation would be structured in a way that maximised tax efficiency and financial flexibility moving forward.

Fergus was excited to see the plan take shape, knowing that the restructured operation would not only save the company a significant amount of money but also provide a solid foundation for the continued growth of Stezland.

After just three years of owning Stezland, Fergus found himself in an unexpectedly good position, with everything falling into place far smoother than he had anticipated. He had settled into the house on the recently subdivided 250-acre parcel of land that he had now dubbed StezPark. This piece of land, once a part of the larger Stezland property, was now his private sanctuary, offering both comfort and space for his growing family and operations.

Wes, who had long been a loyal friend and trusted ally, had transitioned into a more official role as Fergus's personal assistant, as well as his best friend. At Fergus's insistence, Wes had also moved to StezPark, where he lived alongside Fergus and Mitchell. In addition to his role as personal assistant, Wes was now formally the Manager of Stezland Pty Ltd, overseeing the daily operations and ensuring that everything continued to run smoothly.

Mitchell, having completed his schooling, was also living at StezPark. After years of living away during his education, he was delighted to return home and spend more time with his father. He enjoyed the newfound sense of freedom and the cooking of their Vietnamese housekeeper. With a year off before committing to further education, Mitchell decided to pursue a career in veterinary science, having enjoyed working on Stezland the previous year. As a reward for his dedication and work on the property, Fergus decided to make Mitchell the Manager of Stezland Pastoral Pty Ltd, a role that would give him greater responsibility and insight into the family business.

Tim, on the other hand, was still living at the camp in his donga, a simple but content life that suited him well. He had chosen to remain there, and with the title of Manager of Stezland Civil Engineers and Earthmoving Pty Ltd, he was focused on the operations at the camp, managing the earthmoving machinery and civil engineering projects for the business. He was perfectly happy with the arrangement and appreciated the solitude and freedom the camp offered.

Ken had fully settled in as well, having become a permanent resident at the camp. As the accountant for

Stezland Pty Ltd, he had taken over Fergus's office at the camp and was working full-time to manage the financial side of the business. But Ken wasn't all business; he had started brewing his own beer, an endeavour that became quite popular among the camp residents. He began putting the homebrew into kegs and set up a tap in the mess donga, where everyone chipped in by placing money in a jar to help fund the next batch. Mitchell, eager to learn, had picked up the art of home-brewing from Ken and kept StezPark well-stocked with good, kegged, beer for the household.

Meanwhile, the Vietnamese house staff had also adapted to life on Stezland. Bian, the woman in charge of cooking, was excellent at preparing traditional Vietnamese dishes. However, Mitchell, Wes, and Fergus soon found themselves growing weary of the constant diet of Vietnamese food. Taking matters into his own hands, Fergus decided to teach Bian how to prepare more familiar fare. He showed her how to make beef roasts, casseroles, and how to properly cook steaks with crispy chat potatoes on the side. Bian proved to be a fast learner, and before long, the meals had evolved into a more hearty, Western-style menu that was much more to the men's liking.

Bian's husband, Phúc, whom they all affectionately referred to as 'Phúcyoo', had taken up a different sort of challenge. He began to develop a vegetable garden behind the caretaker's unit, but the ground proved to be tough and unyielding. One afternoon, Fergus came home to find Phúc struggling with a post hole shovel, trying to break through the hard earth. Taking matters into his own hands, Fergus borrowed a bobcat from the camp, which was fitted with a rotary hoe and used primarily for creating firebreaks, and showed Phúc how to use the machinery. The next day, Fergus was astonished to find a massive vegetable garden had sprung up, covering nearly 500 square meters. Within just a couple of months, StezPark was graced with fresh vegetables of every variety, growing in accordance with the seasons, providing a steady and healthy supply for the household.

Life at StezPark was thriving. Fergus was content with the progress made on Stezland, with the operations running smoothly, his family and friends surrounding him, and the daily challenges of running the property now seeming more manageable. The entire Stezland operation had come together seamlessly, and the team had successfully created a much-needed service for the local area, particularly with the earthmoving company. This success, however, brought with it an unexpected nuisance, namely, the local Senior Sergeant, who seemed determined to make life difficult for anyone associated with Stezland. He had developed an almost obsessive habit of booking every Stezland Civil Engineering and Earthmoving vehicle he could find. The violations he cited were often for incredibly minor infractions, many of which were common across Cooktown but inexplicably targeted at Stezland's fleet.

Tim, Wes, Ken, and Fergus had found themselves routinely stopped, breathalyzed, and subjected to vehicle defect checks almost every time they entered Cooktown. It had gotten to the point where it was becoming not only a frustration but a serious annoyance. The whole thing was beginning to feel like a campaign against them, and Fergus, increasingly fed up with the situation, confided in Wes one afternoon that he was seriously considering sending a formal complaint to the Queensland Police Commissioner. He thought it might be time to address what he perceived as unfair treatment.

Wes, ever the pragmatic one, advised caution. "Not a good idea, boss," he said with a serious tone. "Because when he goes missing, your letter may become a pointer towards yourself."

Fergus, still slightly incredulous, laughed it off. "I thought you were joking when you spoke about him disappearing."

Wes didn't laugh, though. He thought for a moment before responding, his voice low. "I've thought even more about him disappearing. I have decided the best place would be the quarry floor."

"The quarry floor?" Fergus asked, confused but intrigued.

"Yar, the quarry floor. A hole, a big enough hole to take him and his Landcruiser, dug right here in the quarry. Then you fill it back in. No one's gonna be looking for him there."

Fergus chuckled, dismissing Wes's suggestion as one of his many dark jokes, but the way Wes said it, the casual, matter-of-fact tone, left Fergus with an uneasy feeling. He shook his head, deciding it was all just a bit of hyperbole.

Later that evening, after dinner, Fergus found Mitchell lounging in the lounge, watching a movie. Wes, meanwhile, had set up the pool balls on the snooker table, calling out to Fergus in a tone that seemed to shift into something more casual. "Hey, boss, ready for a game?"

Fergus, still distracted by the earlier conversation, took a moment to walk over and stand beside the table, watching

Wes's methodical setup. The frustrations of the day lingered, but there was something about the quiet in the room that calmed him, for the time being. Yet, the thought of Wes's words about the quarry floor lingered in the back of his mind, half a joke, half a threat. It was hard to shake the idea, and he couldn't help but wonder whether there was more to Wes's comment than just dark humour.

But for now, he pushed those thoughts aside. There was a pool game to be played, and the weight of Stezland's ongoing success, despite the constant interference, was enough to give him a brief respite.

"I am on ze big wons und it's your shot," Wes said with a grin, pouring two glasses of schnapps mixed with coke.

"How could I say no?" Fergus replied, taking the glass Wes handed him. He grabbed his cue from the rack and prepared for his shot. But something lingered in his mind, a question that had been nagging at him ever since Wes had casually mentioned the quarry.

"How would the Sergeant and his car get to the quarry without being seen?" Fergus asked, his voice light but probing.

Wes let out a laugh, a deep, knowing chuckle. "That is called, vorks in progress," he said cryptically, with a wink.

Fergus chuckled along with him, but in that moment, something in Wes's demeanour shifted, his smile didn't quite reach his eyes. Fergus suddenly realised that Senior Sergeant Sutton's antics had stirred up more in Wes than he initially understood. The playful tone didn't fool him anymore. Wes had been deeply affected by the constant harassment, and his earlier comments about Sutton 'disappearing' now seemed less like a joke and more like a warning.

Fergus's mind, trained from years of military discipline, recognised the danger in Wes's words and actions. There was a side to Wes that few people ever saw, the side that could be coldly calculated and ruthlessly effective when pushed too far. He had always respected Wes for his loyalty and unflappable nature, but the thought of the Sergeant's taunts, particularly when Sutton had boldly declared that "no one would ever take my gun from me" at the station, made the situation feel much more dangerous. Wes had taken that as a direct challenge, a gauntlet thrown down without the Sergeant even realising it.

Fergus knew enough about military protocol to understand that such words, coming from someone like Sutton, were more than just idle threats. They were a declaration of dominance, a power play that could have far-reaching consequences. But what Sutton didn't know was that, in challenging Wes in such a manner, he had inadvertently issued a challenge not only to a man's authority but to his very pride.

The fool Sergeant had no idea how deeply his words had cut. He might as well have slapped Wes across the face with a gauntlet, the same way duels were challenged in days of old. Fergus could see it now, Wes was a man who didn't take such slights lightly. And in that moment, Fergus's earlier dismissals of Wes's words began to fade.

Sutton's actions had, without a doubt, provoked something in Wes that could become a very dangerous situation.

The New March

.

Max Barrington

Over the past few weeks, Fergus and Wes had started noticing an increasing number of vehicles passing by the quarry, heading towards the 'Y' road intersection. Whenever these individuals were intercepted at either the camp or the 'Gatehouse,' they would offer the same excuse: they had gotten lost while trying to access the beach near Bloomfield, only to end up on the wrong road heading toward Whalebone Beach.

Intrigued by the repeated misdirection, Fergus and Wes decided to investigate further. They set out together, driving across towards the tracks from Whalebone Beach that intersected with the quarry road. After surveying the tracks, they quickly concluded that the path was of no use to them. A better road was already in place, one that came onto the Whale Beach road but was blocked by a locked gate they had installed for cattle transportation. It seemed like an ideal solution to keep people from accidentally wandering onto Stezland, so they decided to shut down the route entirely.

However, as they explored further, they discovered a section of the track running along a narrow batter on the side of a steep hill. It was an exposed spot, where any vehicle trying to navigate the track would be precariously close to a high cliff. This seemed like the perfect place to implement a more permanent solution.

Fergus and Wes quickly came up with a plan: they would use the Air Track Drill and Compressor from the quarry to drill a series of holes along the hillside. The plan was to charge the holes with Ammonium Nitrate mixed with diesel, turning the concoction into a paste that would then be detonated to block off the path entirely.

The following morning, they spent hours transporting the Air Track and Compressor to the selected site, a job that took longer than expected. By two o'clock that afternoon, they had finally set all four charges into place, carefully priming them before stepping back to watch the show. Moments later, the hillside erupted in a massive explosion, sending rocks and debris tumbling down into the valley below, creating a huge void where the track had once been. The path was completely obliterated, leaving no chance for anyone to follow it in the future.

Satisfied with their work, they made their way back to the quarry, planning to return the equipment. The task had taken longer than expected, and it was well into the evening by the time they were ready to head back, the rumble of the Air Track's engine echoing through the night as they made their way back to base. The job was done, Stezland's privacy was secured, and anyone who might venture too close would find themselves well and truly lost.

The time had come for Stezland's second cattle muster, but this year they were ready to handle it themselves. No contractors were needed now, as the self-mustering gates they had installed in the extended holding yard were operational. The process was straightforward: they simply had to close the gates so they opened inward toward the enclosure. With a spring mechanism on each gate, they would automatically close behind the cattle once they entered, preventing them from escaping. It was a simple yet effective system, allowing the cattle to freely wander in without the need for any chasing or prodding, which had made musters in the past so much more challenging.

The timing was perfect, as this was just months before the wet season, and most of the waterholes and small creeks had dried up. At this point, the cattle had become familiar with drinking from the troughs placed in the enclosures, which Mitchell maintained regularly. The self-mustering gates, at this time of year, remained locked in the open position, allowing the cattle to move freely between the enclosures without any restriction. But as muster time drew near, everything changed.

The routine for the muster was set: for three days, they would fill the round bale hay handlers with fresh hay, drawing the cattle in slowly. They counted the cattle each day, and after four days, the numbers plateaued. They assumed they had gathered them all, as there were far more cattle this year, and without the need for men on horseback chasing them, the cattle moved freely into the enclosures, not attempting to evade capture.

Mitchell quickly realised, however, that the cattle weren't as docile as they appeared. Even the small heifers, typically more skittish, had started charging at him for no apparent reason, and he had to learn how to handle their unpredictable behaviour with care.

This year, they were also tasked with bringing back the bulls and replacing some of the older ones. Colin had instructed them to buy six new bulls, two for each of the runs, as he recommended replacing bulls every two years in each run. He also suggested a maximum lifespan of seven years for any bull, which was a guideline they planned to follow strictly.

The 'Freebody' ramp, which had already proven invaluable, needed just a couple more modifications to make it even more efficient. It had worked perfectly for loading the cattle, but there was always room for improvement, and they were determined to get it just right.

In addition to these changes, Fergus had also made a significant investment: a bogey-drive R-series Mack truck with a double-decker cattle carrier B-double trailer. The trailer was equipped with folding interlocking decks, allowing both trailers to be loaded simultaneously without needing to disconnect them. This new rig would be used to transport cattle from the muster yards to the camp yard, saving time and effort during the transfer process. The prime mover would also be used to move the 'Freebody' ramp to each of the muster yards as needed, adding even more versatility to the operation.

With everything in place, the muster was shaping up to be a much smoother process than before, and Fergus felt confident that the improvements they had made would lead to a more efficient and successful operation in the years to come. Mitchell had taken the initiative to visit a neighbouring property to learn the proper techniques for marking (castrating) the male calves, making this task officially his responsibility going forward. In addition to marking, Mitchell also took on the important job of dehorning the calves to ensure the herd would be manageable and safe for handling. Meanwhile, Wes handled the ear tagging process, ensuring each animal was properly identified for future reference and tracking.

This year, the number of bullocks ready for the market had increased slightly, reaching a total of 201 animals. The sale price per head was also a pleasant surprise, with each bullock fetching $1,006. This was a welcome improvement over previous years. However, the transport costs to Charters Towers remained high, totalling $19,000, which was in line with last year's expenses.

After subtracting transport costs, the gross income from the sale of the cattle came to $183,206. From that amount, Stezland had to offset charges to other Stezland subsidiaries, equipment and land leases, services, and other internal allocations, amounting to approximately $175,000. This left a taxable net profit of about $10,000, which was just below the tax threshold, sparing them from any significant tax obligations for the year.

Fergus had started to seriously consider investing in a fleet of B Double trailers, or even road trains, along with prime movers, as a way to both cut down on his own cattle transport costs and generate additional revenue by offering transport services to other businesses. He had noticed a significant shortage of stock transport vehicles in the area, and the long lead times for booking transport, often requiring reservations six months in advance, were causing headaches for local producers. This presented an opportunity for Fergus to capitalise on the situation by owning and operating his own fleet.

However, his enthusiasm quickly waned after conducting some research into the logistics and regulations surrounding cattle transportation in the region. He discovered that cattle could only be transported for a maximum of 48 hours before they needed to be unloaded for a break. This was even more problematic in Far North Queensland's intense heat, where the animals could endure less time on the road due to the risk of overheating and stress. Not only did this create a bottleneck in the logistics, but it also added unnecessary complexity to the entire process.

Another significant hurdle was the challenge of finding suitable, dedicated drivers who could handle the responsibility of transporting cattle over long distances. The drivers needed to be skilled cattlemen, capable of managing both the animals' welfare and the mechanics of driving heavy transport rigs. Unfortunately, Fergus learned that while there were plenty of transport vehicles available in the region, many of them were idle due to a shortage of skilled drivers. This lack of experienced, reliable personnel made it clear that running a fleet would not be as simple or profitable as he had hoped.

Realising the logistical and human resource challenges involved, Fergus reluctantly decided to put the idea of investing in a fleet of trucks on hold. The reality of the complexities surrounding cattle transportation in the region left him with little desire to dive into the business, at least for the time being.

Fergus was in the middle of his daily routine when he received an unexpected call from the Cooktown Council's road maintenance section. The voice on the other end was slightly hurried, as if the caller had been trying to reach him for some time.

"Mr. Laird, this is Howard Johnston from the roads maintenance section at Cooktown Council," the man said.

Fergus, slightly distracted, assumed the call was about something routine. "I think you're looking for Tim Abbott," he replied. "He handles all the road maintenance for your council. I can give you his office number, and if he's not there, you can leave a message."

He was about to hang up, but Howard Johnston quickly interrupted him, his voice more insistent now.

"No! No, Mr. Laird, please listen carefully," the council worker continued, sounding urgent. "It's about one of the gazetted roads on your property. It's been severely damaged."

Fergus paused, his attention piqued. "Gazetted road?" he asked, confused. "I don't have any gazetted roads on Stezland."

Howard Johnston, now with a tone of clear concern, fully described the location of the damaged road. As the details rolled off his tongue, Fergus's memory clicked, and he instantly recognised the road in question. It was the same one where he and Wes had taken measures to block access by erasing a section along the hillside. Fergus had made the decision to alter the road to prevent unauthorised people from entering private property, but he hadn't considered that it was a gazetted road, meaning it was a publicly recognised thoroughfare.

"I didn't realise it was a gazetted road," Fergus admitted, quickly understanding the gravity of the situation. "I had no idea it was an official road," he continued, his voice calm but now acknowledging the possible consequences of his actions.

Howard Johnston, clearly frustrated, asked, "Why would you destroy it?"

Fergus paused for a moment, gathering his thoughts before responding honestly. "I did it to stop people from entering the property. It wasn't meant to cause any damage or harm, but just to prevent trespassers from using that route to access Stezland."

There was a brief silence on the other end of the line before Howard Johnston responded, his voice a bit softer but still firm. "Mr. Laird, regardless of your reasons, altering a gazetted road without permission is a serious matter. You'll need to fix the damage and restore the road. We'll be sending someone out to assess the situation."

Fergus listened intently as the council man on the other end of the line spoke, his voice measured but still firm. "Mr. Laird, I must inform you that you cannot simply stop people from entering private property if there is a gazetted road running through it," Howard Johnston explained. "However, people on that road have no right to leave it and trespass onto your property."

Fergus raised an eyebrow, processing the information. He had assumed that blocking the road had been within his rights, but now it seemed like he would need a more compelling reason to keep people away. The council man's tone softened slightly. "If you want to prevent access to your property on this road, you'll need to have a very good reason, something like health and safety concerns. Would you have any reasons that fit that criteria?"

Fergus thought for a moment, considering the possibilities. A smile crept across his face as a potential solution formed in his mind. "Hmmm... yes, certainly," he said, feeling a sense of confidence. "That road leads to the quarry. If someone were to come down that road while we were blasting, it would be extremely dangerous."

He waited for the council man's response, convinced that this would be a valid reason to prevent access. But instead of the agreement he expected, the line went quiet for a beat. Then Howard Johnston's voice returned, this time tinged with surprise.

"Sorry... did you say a quarry?" he asked, his tone now more cautious.

"Yes," Fergus replied, a little taken aback by the question. "We have two quarries on Stezland. That's where we source all the road materials we provide to your council."

There was a long pause on the other end of the line, and Fergus could almost hear the council man's mind processing the new information. "I'll have to get back to you, Mr. Laird," Howard Johnston said after a moment. "There's no mention of a quarry on the property description. I'll need to check why that hasn't been updated. Apologies for the trouble, and I'll find out what's going on. Goodbye."

Fergus stared at the phone for a moment, feeling both frustrated and somewhat bemused. The quarry, which had been a key part of Stezland's operations, wasn't even listed in the official property records. It seemed like another bureaucratic oversight that could now complicate matters. He wasn't sure what the council man would find, but it was clear that this would delay any action Fergus had hoped to take.

With a resigned sigh, Fergus set the phone down and began mentally preparing for the next round of red tape. The conversation with the council had left Fergus feeling uneasy. He had a nagging suspicion that the phone call was just the beginning of a much larger issue, one he hadn't anticipated. He decided to call Ken, hoping for some insight, but after explaining the situation, Ken couldn't offer much advice. The more Fergus thought about it, the more he realised that something serious was brewing. Finally, he reached out to his solicitor, Brian Haptu, hoping for some clarity.

"Are you telling me, Fergus, that you didn't apply for permits from the Department of Mineral Resources before you started quarrying?" Brian's voice came through the line, stern and surprised.

Fergus paused. "No, I didn't know I had to. It's on my land, why would I need their permission? Fuck them," he muttered, his frustration mounting.

Brian let out a sigh. "Well, that's a problem, isn't it?"

Soon after, a heated discussion unfolded between Fergus, Wes, Tim, Ken, and Brian. They all gathered at StezPark to hash out the situation and figure out how to tackle the mess Fergus had inadvertently created. The mood was tense, with every suggestion seeming to spiral into more complications.

Brian was the first to act. He immediately registered an application with the Queensland Department of Mines and Energy, submitting a detailed location description of the quarry. To no one's surprise, the application was promptly declined. The department cited that the area in question contained protected Remnant Vegetation, a critical part of the local ecosystem, and could not be disturbed. Worse still, any mining or quarrying activity in the area had to cease within thirty days, and the area itself had to be completely sealed off from all access.

Fergus was stunned. "I appreciate it's your land, Fergus, but sadly, you can't just do as you please with it," Brian said, his tone sympathetic but firm. "I've researched the area thoroughly. A lot of the tracks around Stezland are actually gazetted roads, which complicates things further. This area was once covered by mining leases, but once mining ceased and the environmental damage was revealed, the Federal Government stepped in and banned any further mining or quarrying in the area."

Brian paused for a moment, letting the weight of the situation sink in. "End of story, Fergus. This is one battle you're not going to win, and I strongly urge you not to push it."

Fergus sat back, his mind racing. He hadn't considered the implications of mining regulations, protected land, and gazetted roads. He felt a mixture of disbelief and regret, he had assumed that because it was his land, he could do whatever he wanted. But now, he was facing a situation that was far more complicated than he had ever anticipated.

Tim, who had been quietly listening, spoke up. "I've found another location. A much more suitable area with some really good deposits of road-building materials," he said. "We could easily shift operations there, no problem."

After some reflection, Fergus finally agreed. It was time to accept the reality of the situation. He admitted, somewhat reluctantly, that he had never even considered the need for permits or the intricacies of gazetted roads. "I guess I'm going to have to do as I'm told for once," he said, his voice tinged with frustration but also acceptance. "I'll reinstate the road I destroyed."

The group spent the next few hours discussing how to handle the restoration of the damaged road and the necessary steps to shift their quarrying operation to a new location. The decision wasn't easy for Fergus, but he knew it was the only way forward. Despite the setbacks, he would have to play by the rules this time, something he wasn't used to doing, but ultimately, it was the only option left.

As the meeting concluded, Fergus reflected on the lesson he had just learned: sometimes, even the most well-intentioned decisions can have unintended consequences, and the weight of bureaucracy can crush even the most confident business owner. But he was determined to move forward, knowing that Stezland's future depended on adapting to the rules rather than defying them.

A Plan

Wes and Fergus were engaged in another heated game of pool, a routine that had become quite common in the evenings. The game seemed to flow better with a glass or two of schnapps and coke, something Wes had introduced to Fergus over time. The pool table became a haven for the two of them, a place to unwind after the day's hard work and discuss whatever was on their minds.

"Ve need a back gate," Wes said suddenly, breaking the silence as he took a shot.

"A back gate? For what?" Fergus asked, absentmindedly setting up his next shot.

"You cannot drive here into this home without everyone at ze camp or za 'Gatehouse' seeing you," Wes replied matter-of-factly, looking over at Fergus with a raised brow.

Fergus paused for a moment, contemplating the idea. "Does it matter if people see you driving past the camp?" he asked.

"If you are driving a police car up to the quarry, then yar!" Wes replied with a grin, his eyes twinkling with mischief.

Fergus laughed, shaking his head. "Are you still thinking about that copper disappearing?"

"Und you are not?" Wes looked at him, a hint of confusion in his eyes. "You are not thinking of it seriously, Fergus?"

Fergus leaned on his cue stick, letting out a long breath. "I don't hate him enough to kill him," he said, the words coming slowly. "But he is a real pain in the arse. I've had enough of him. I wish I had killed the other mongrel,

Kirkland, when I had the chance a couple of years ago. I've got a lot to hate him for."

Wes gave a slight nod, as if he understood the depths of Fergus's frustrations. "Yar, maybe you will get another chance now he is back in Cooktown."

Fergus stopped mid-shot, the cue stick frozen in his hands. He turned to Wes, his expression suddenly serious. "What? What are you saying?" His voice was low, a tinge of alarm in it.

Wes casually took another sip of his schnapps and coke before answering. "I saw Sutton on Charlotte Street yesterday. Kirkland was with him. It looked like Kirkland has three stripes on his arm now."

Fergus was stunned. He sat down heavily on the nearby chair, his mind racing. "I can't believe it. Kirkland's back in Cooktown?" His voice was filled with disbelief. The idea of Kirkland returning seemed almost impossible, especially after everything that had happened in the past.

Wes shrugged, a grim smile on his face. "Yar, looks like it. Guess you've got some unfinished business with him after all."

Fergus sat there for a moment, the weight of Wes's words sinking in. The idea of Kirkland back in town, especially in some kind of official capacity, brought back a flood of memories. Fergus had hoped to never see the man again, but now that he knew Kirkland was back, the old animosity was stirring once more. There were unfinished scores to settle, and now it seemed that fate had handed him an opportunity.

The New March

It was late afternoon the following day when Wes took Fergus for a drive in his FJ40, winding through the dense landscape behind the house. They manoeuvred around trees and rocks, the soft rumble of the Landcruiser the only sound breaking the peaceful silence. After what felt like an eternity of navigating the rugged terrain, they finally arrived at an unnamed creek. It lay just below, but out of sight from the house, about three kilometres away by Fergus's estimation.

They parked the Landcruiser almost at the water's edge, and Wes, always prepared, pulled out a topographical map. They stepped out of the vehicle, the sun casting long shadows over the creek's flowing water.

"The camp cattle yards are just around there, about a kilometre," Wes said, gesturing toward the bend in the creek.

Fergus squinted in the direction Wes pointed, shaking his head in disbelief. "No way," he muttered under his breath.

With a resigned sigh, they walked a few steps back to the Landcruiser, and Wes unfolded the map, spreading it out on the hood for a better look. He pointed at the map, tracing the route with his finger.

"Look here," Wes said, highlighting the creek and the hill to their right when facing the water. "See, just around this hill here, yar?"

Fergus's eyes followed the path, then widened in astonishment. "Can't be... can it?" He paused, taking in the information as if seeing the landscape in a new light. "Well, fuck me," he muttered, almost to himself. He was taken aback, realising how wrong his perception had been. The house, which he had always thought to be nestled at the base of the massive hills, was actually positioned behind one of those hills, closer to the camp and the 'Gatehouse'. The impression of being at the base of the hills came from the drive past the 'Gatehouse,' where the road veered into a gorge, leading him back in a large circle without him ever realising it.

"Now, komm look at this, boss," Wes said with enthusiasm, leading Fergus toward a huge boulder about three meters high and five meters wide, partially submerged in the creek. They approached it from the right, and as they walked past the boulder and peered across the creek, their view was blocked by another massive boulder. This one was even bigger, at about seven meters long, with the same height as the first.

Wes turned to Fergus, his face serious now. "You vill need to take off your boots here, and socks, and roll up your trousers," he said with a grin.

Fergus groaned. "Is this necessary?"

"Komm und look," Wes insisted, already kicking off his boots and rolling up his trousers to his knees.

Reluctantly, Fergus followed suit, slipping off his boots and rolling up his pants. He stepped into the cool water, walking behind Wes as they moved through the gap between the two enormous boulders. The space between the rocks was about two and a half meters wide, and they continued upstream until they cleared the larger boulder. From here, they could see the bank on the opposite side.

Wes kept walking, almost to the far bank, and then stopped, turning around to face Fergus. "Turn around," he instructed.

Fergus did as he was told and was instantly amazed. From his new vantage point, the two boulders appeared to have merged into one massive rock, and the gap between them was now completely hidden. As he walked along the water, up to his left, he realised that the unique angle of the first boulder completely obscured the second. The more he looked, the more it seemed like the rocks had been positioned to create a seamless natural barrier.

"Now komm this way," Wes called to him, leading him further down the creek.

They waded through the water, up to their knees now, walking past the boulders. About one kilometre further, the creek curved around in a long bend, and Fergus could make out a shallow crossing in the water, a crossing he had never noticed before, despite it being so close to the 'Gatehouse' and camp.

"Das will be our back gate, yar?" Wes grinned, looking over at Fergus.

Fergus stood in awe, considering the possibilities. The idea of a back gate at this crossing had potential, but he knew it would take some work to turn it into a practical entry point. He had been contemplating creating a low-level concrete crossing for some time now, something that would allow vehicles to cross without getting their tires wet, thus avoiding the accumulation of mud on the wheels and in the wheel arches. The idea of having a more efficient and clean way to navigate between the camp and the house was appealing, especially when the roads were at their dustiest.

As he watched the water flow gently past the boulders, Fergus realised how much potential this spot had. The back gate idea was solid, it just required the right kind of work to bring it to life. With Wes's knack for finding hidden solutions and Fergus's drive to improve the property, it seemed like the perfect project for the both of them.

Fergus had spent the last few days working on the design for the concrete crossing. He had carefully calculated the materials, labor, and the associated costs, and after running through the numbers, he came to a conclusion that gave him pause. The final estimate was far higher than he had anticipated. The cost of constructing the crossing, while necessary, seemed excessive for what it would provide, a simple, low-level concrete crossing to allow vehicles to pass without the inconvenience of getting their tires wet.

But then, as he sat there pondering the cost, a memory surfaced. It was a time not long ago when he had made another investment that, at the time, had seemed similarly extravagant. Fergus had recalled the moment he'd bought a new Toyota Prado, a vehicle that would serve as the company car for trips to Cooktown and, occasionally, Mareeba and Cairns. The decision had been made to ease his own workload, so he wouldn't have to take his own trusty Land Rover on the longer trips. He'd assigned the Prado to Ken, his right-hand man, who often handled the local transport tasks and deliveries.

Ken had been absolutely thrilled when he received the Prado. He'd practically beamed with excitement when

Fergus handed over the keys. "Boss, this is the best job in the world!" Ken had said, his voice filled with gratitude. "And I reckon I live in the best place in the world." It had been one of those moments that made all the hard work and business decisions worthwhile for Fergus. Ken's enthusiasm and appreciation had been palpable, a reminder that the decisions he made had a positive impact on the team, even if they sometimes seemed like hefty investments at first.

As Fergus sat in the quiet of his office, his mind drifting between the present project and the past memory, he realised that perhaps the cost of the concrete crossing wasn't as much of a burden as it first appeared. Just as the Prado had turned out to be an investment in efficiency and employee satisfaction, the crossing could prove to be the same, a long-term investment that would improve access to the property, reduce wear and tear on vehicles, and, in time, pay for itself. Sometimes, the best decisions were the ones that didn't seem immediately practical but made sense in the broader picture.

He leaned back in his chair, taking a moment to let the thought settle in. The concrete crossing would be a worthwhile expense. After all, it wasn't just about the immediate costs, it was about improving the infrastructure of the land, enhancing efficiency, and making life easier for everyone who worked there. The project now seemed less like an extravagance and more like the necessary step forward it was always meant to be.

It had only been two days since Fergus had handed over the keys to the Prado to Ken, a gesture he'd hoped would make his employee's job easier and add to his sense of appreciation for the work he did. But when Ken returned from the banking trip to Cooktown, his demeanour was far from the bright, grateful attitude he'd shown when first receiving the vehicle. Fergus found him at his house, and the sorrow in Ken's eyes was impossible to ignore. With a heavy heart, Ken broke the news that he was leaving his job.

Fergus was utterly stunned. He hadn't expected this turn of events at all. "What's going on, Ken?" he asked, his voice thick with confusion and concern. "Why the sudden decision? You were just getting settled."

Ken explained with a deep sigh, the weight of his words hanging heavy in the air. "Sutton pulled me over this morning in Cooktown. He told me he was going to have my parole revoked. He said I was consorting with a convicted criminal, meaning you, Fergus."

Fergus felt a surge of anger and disbelief. He quickly dismissed the accusation. "That's complete bullshit. You know that consorting doesn't apply if it's just the two of us. It has to be three convicted criminals for that to even count."

But Ken wasn't convinced. His face showed the fear and uncertainty that Fergus knew all too well. "I don't care, Fergus. Sutton's got it out for me, and I can't risk going back to prison. No way. I won't survive that again."

Fergus was crushed. He couldn't fathom the possibility of losing Ken, especially after everything they'd built together. He spent the next several hours trying to reason with him, making phone calls to their mutual contacts. One of those calls was to Brian Haptu, who had been a steady source of support for both Fergus and Ken over the years. Brian had immediately given Ken the phone number of a barrister who could help.

The barrister, after hearing Ken's case, had reassured him that the chances of his parole being revoked were slim, especially given his current role in the community and his work with Fergus. It would be highly unusual for someone in Ken's position to face such a consequence, especially considering the good standing he had earned since being released. The legal expert's calm and confident words finally started to sink in for Ken, easing some of the fear and uncertainty that had gripped him.

Still, the whole ordeal had been nerve-wracking for both of them. Not only was it a potential disaster for Fergus on the business side, but it would have been utterly heartbreaking for Ken. The emotional toll of possibly returning to prison weighed heavily on him, and Fergus couldn't bear the thought of his friend being caught in such a cruel situation.

Having lived through the intensity of that moment, Fergus knew he couldn't let anything jeopardise their progress now. He took a deep breath, clearing his mind and focusing on the work at hand. He turned his attention back to the concrete crossing project he had started designing. The experience with Ken had reminded him of the importance of securing the future, not just for his business, but for the people around him.

With a newfound sense of resolve, Fergus finished the design for the low-level crossing and handed it over to Tim, instructing him to begin work on it as soon as possible. He also made plans to survey the creek for a temporary diversion the following day, which would facilitate both the construction of the crossing and the secretive "back gate" road project.

This would be a critical part of the overall work, one that needed to be kept under wraps for now. The "back gate" was a key piece of the puzzle, and Fergus had no intention of letting anyone interfere with the project, especially after everything that had happened with Ken.

Fergus had tracked down Wes and told him that they would be surveying the creek for a temporary diversion the next day.

"Fucking ripper!" Wes had exclaimed, clearly excited by the prospect. He immediately suggested a game of pool after dinner to celebrate.

The task at hand was straightforward. Due to the wide span of the creek, around twenty meters between the banks, the diversion wasn't going to be too complicated. One of Tim's top operators from Hope Vale, who was known for handling big machinery with precision, had been assigned to operate the large Cat excavator at Fergus's request. The decision to use someone other than Jason, the usual operator, had been made for a very specific reason. Fergus didn't want Jason to see the boulder formation where they intended to build the StezPark 'back gate.' It wasn't that he thought Jason would cause any trouble, but Fergus preferred to keep the details of the 'back gate' project as secret as possible. The fewer people who knew about it, the better.

To make sure the project ran smoothly, Fergus also leased a portable 'dry batch' concrete plant from Mount Isa. Along with the plant, he secured two concrete agitator trucks, fitted with Mack R600 6WD ex-army trucks. These vehicles would be crucial in the coming days, and Fergus was hands-on in managing them. To support the concrete production, he purchased a Michigan articulated 4WD front-end loader with a three-meter, four-way bucket. This loader was tasked with moving sand and gravel taken from the creek bed below, just downstream from where the diversion was set to be constructed.

The work began in earnest, and it quickly became a source of amusement for the other workers. Although everyone else had finished their day's work, Fergus and Wes would sometimes work into the late afternoon, mixing and pouring around seventy cubic meters of concrete directly onto the course riverbed. Their task was to fill in the swirl holes, each about two meters wide, from the centre of the proposed concrete span and extending up towards the massive boulders.

It was labor-intensive, but they managed it with ease, working together in a rhythm that only years of experience could bring. They poured the concrete carefully, ensuring a smooth, steady flow.

By the time the evening set in and the other workers were heading back to the camp, Fergus and Wes would leave the site. They would return early the next morning, before the first rays of light had even touched the land. Using two bobcats, they spread a thin layer of river gravel and sand over the freshly poured concrete. The goal was to make it appear as though nothing had been done, leaving the work completely invisible to anyone who might happen by during the day.

The secrecy and precision with which Fergus and Wes handled the task were paramount. They knew the importance of keeping things under wraps, especially as the project took shape. And so, each day, they repeated the process, working late into the night and early in the morning, creating a flawless camouflage for the work they had done.

"So, my friend," said Fergus to Wes, both of them still up and playing pool after dinner. Their evening had been fuelled by more than a few of Mitchell's beers and a couple of Schnapps. "The 'back gate' is finished. Tell me more about your plans, how does our target get taken?"

Wes, who had been eyeing the cue ball with precision, paused and looked at Fergus. "He lives in his house on Flinders Street," he began, his voice steady, though there was a cold edge to it. "It's a very leafy, almost bush-like street. And though it's only about three hundred meters from the police station, he drives to and from there every day, almost at the exact time, five forty-five PM."

Fergus raised an eyebrow, cutting Wes off. "Sounds like you've been stalking him."

Wes shrugged casually. "It wasn't hard to find this out. Didn't take much time at all, but it's here, at his home, in the evening, that I'd take him out. I'd shoot him while he's still in his car, and then drive him about five hundred meters further along Flinders Street. That's where it's just bush, and I'll have the 'tilt tray' stock truck parked there. We drive the police car onto the stock truck, head out of town, and back to our causeway. We unload the vehicle, go through the 'back gate,' up to the quarry, and down into the hole. Fill the hole, and... voila."

Fergus stared at him, his mind racing. "Fuck me, Wes, you've really got this worked out, haven't you? You're serious about this."

Wes didn't flinch. "He's ruining things for us, Fergus. He's made it personal. He's upset Ken... and soon, he'll be picking on Mitchell. He's just a cunt. He has to go." He paused, then added with a dark grin, "But I think we should also get rid of the other prick at the same time... if we can come up with a plan. There's plenty of room in Sutton's police car."

Fergus took a deep breath. "Where does Kirkland live?"

Wes sighed, looking slightly defeated. "That's the problem. He lives out of town, and I haven't come up with a plan for him yet... but I will."

Fergus shook his head, rubbing his eyes as he poured them both another round of Mitchell's kegged beer. "So, the copper arrives home in his car at five forty-five, and then what?"

Wes leaned forward, his voice lowering even further. "The moment he opens the car door, I shoot him before he gets out. That's very important, because if he gets out, shooting him would be difficult. He's a fat prick, weighs over a hundred kilos, and getting him from the ground back into the car would be a lot of work. So, he must be shot while still in the car."

Fergus raised an eyebrow. "And... no one would hear the shot? A rifle? Or a shotgun, maybe?"

Wes smirked, revealing a glimpse of something far darker. "I have a special weapon made for such jobs. It's been kept from the KSK, and I smuggled it into Australia by disassembling it and hiding the parts in my luggage. I'll show you."

With a deliberate air, Wes left the snooker room, returning shortly with a polished timber box. He placed it carefully on the pool table, as though it held something far more valuable than just a weapon. He opened the box to reveal a Russian-manufactured Margolin .22 target pistol, nestled in a red velvet mould.

Wes took the pistol in his hands, worked the cocking slide with ease, and then handed it to Fergus. "Take a look," he said.

Fergus examined it closely, admiring the sleek design. "Wow... looks impressive," he muttered, handing it back to Wes.

Wes didn't respond immediately. Instead, he unscrewed a knurled cap from the top of the barrel, revealing a fine thread. He took a small cylindrical object from the box, holding it up as he murmured, "Suppressor." He attached it carefully, then inserted one of the fully loaded magazines into the pistol. With a practiced motion, he cocked it, making it ready to fire.

Wes walked over to a lounge chair and picked up one of the hand-sewn red leather cushions that Bian had made. With a steady hand, he placed the barrel of the Margolin against the cushion and fired.

Fergus, expecting a louder noise, was taken aback when he heard nothing but a faint click. He had assumed the weapon had misfired, but then saw the empty .22 case eject from the pistol, still confused. Wes held up the cushion, showing the tiny entry hole left by the projectile. Despite the cushion being misshapen and likely permanently distorted, there was no exit hole, the .22 round was still embedded inside it.

"Fuck me!" exclaimed Fergus, staring at the cushion in disbelief before shifting his gaze back to the pistol. His mind was reeling, he was no stranger to firearms, having grown up around them and having a deep respect for their power. But this? This was something else entirely. The weapon was silent, almost eerily so, and there was no mess, just the calm aftermath of a single, precise shot. It was far more sinister than anything he had encountered before.

Wes, seeming almost detached as he admired the pistol in his hand, explained in a calm, matter-of-fact tone, "The Margolin is standard issue in the KSK, along with a Walther 9mm. The Margolin's designed specifically for silent close-combat situations, where discretion is the priority. It's not about making noise, it's about efficiency and precision. It doesn't leave a trace."

Fergus's mind raced. The KSK was the German Army's elite special forces, known for their brutal efficiency and ability to operate covertly in the most dangerous environments. If this weapon was their standard issue, then it was more than just a tool, it was a testament to the kind of operations Wes was prepared for.

As Wes spoke, Fergus couldn't help but feel the weight of the situation pressing down on him. It was clear now: Wes wasn't just talking about a plan; he was talking about an execution. Every element of the operation seemed to be meticulously thought out, as if he had already lived it in his mind a thousand times over. From the timing of the target's arrival home, to the method of extraction, to the use of the "back gate", every detail was accounted for.

Fergus knew better than to doubt Wes's abilities. This wasn't the kind of plan you could dismiss with a laugh or a shake of the head. There was an unsettling confidence in Wes's demeanour that spoke volumes. No matter what question Fergus threw at him, Wes had a calm, perfect answer. He wasn't just going through the motions, he was operating on a level that seemed almost invincible.

And that was the part that unsettled Fergus the most: it wasn't just that Wes had everything planned; it was the certainty in his eyes, the cold, methodical approach he took to every step. In that moment, Fergus realised that Wes was fully committed to seeing this through, and the consequences of that commitment would be far-reaching, no matter the outcome.

Fergus glanced at the Margolin again. The silence of the shot, the quiet precision, it wasn't just a weapon; it was a promise. And as much as he had hoped to keep some distance from this darker side of things, he now found himself pulled deeper into the web.

"Wes," Fergus said slowly, breaking the silence, his voice quieter than usual, "You've got this all figured out, don't you?"

Wes nodded, his eyes never leaving the weapon in his hand. "I do," he said simply, his voice low and steady. "And it will be done."

Fergus had no doubt.

The form-workers had meticulously completed the layout for the causeway, carefully positioning the five 300-millimetre diameter pipes that ran through the centre of the structure. These pipes would allow for water to flow underneath the causeway, ensuring that the top surface remained dry and stable under normal conditions. It was a critical part of the design, one that would help prevent flooding and erosion, keeping the road accessible even during periods of heavy rain.

Fergus and Wes, having spent long hours preparing and delivering the concrete, were now watching as the contract concrete placers worked to finish the surface of the causeway. The smooth, gray slab was slowly taking shape, its surface polished and level, a testament to the care and precision that had gone into its creation. The work was hard and often painstaking, but the satisfaction of seeing the causeway coming together made every moment worth it.

The owner of the mobile concrete plant and its fleet of trucks was now on his way to collect the equipment, which would be transported back to Mount Isa. It had been a productive operation, but the time had come for everything to be packed up and moved. With the causeway nearing completion, Wes decided it was time to focus on the next task at hand, digging the hole in the quarry.

Stezland now boasted two quarries, each serving a distinct purpose. The first quarry, once a hub of activity, had now fallen into disuse except for the large stockpiles of crushed deco that lay dormant, waiting for the occasional project that required it. The second quarry, however, was where the real action was taking place. Situated roughly one kilometre away from the first, this quarry had recently been fitted with a crushing plant designed to process a much higher-quality road base. This new road base met the stringent requirements of the local council, making it an invaluable resource for the growing demands of road construction and maintenance.

It was the first quarry, the older one, that Wes had chosen as the final resting place for Sutton and his car, as well as Kirkland, if he could find a way to deal with them both at once. It was the perfect location, remote and hidden from view, surrounded by the vast expanse of Stezland's rugged terrain. The quarry had been a place of hard labor and gritty work, but now, it was going to serve a much darker purpose, one that would tie up loose ends and solve problems that had been simmering for far too long.

Wes knew what needed to be done, and he had a plan. He had already made arrangements to borrow the Cat excavator and a tip truck for the task at hand, but there was one problem, Tim. The excavator had been in use for more than a week already, working on the creek diversion channel and other contract jobs that Tim had lined up. These projects were critical, and Tim simply couldn't afford to lose the excavator for a couple more days. His business relied on it, and delays were becoming costly.

Despite the inconvenience, Tim knew he couldn't say no to Wes. The bond between Wes and Fergus was unbreakable, and Wes was more than just an employee or a trusted colleague. He was like a brother to Fergus, and that carried weight. So, Tim reluctantly agreed to make a request to Fergus, knowing that if anyone could smooth things over and make this work, it would be him.

Tim approached Fergus with a sense of unease. The request was difficult, but he needed the excavator for his own projects, and he wasn't sure how to navigate the delicate situation. Fergus, always the pragmatic one, listened attentively as Tim explained the predicament. After a long pause, Fergus looked up from his work and met Tim's eyes, understanding the dilemma.

"I'll see what I can do," Fergus said, his voice calm but resolute. He wasn't happy about the delay in Tim's projects, but he knew the importance of what Wes had planned, and the urgency of it all. It wasn't just about the excavator, it was about getting things done the right way, no matter what.

Tim had briefly explained the situation to Fergus regarding Wes's request to use the excavator, but Fergus, ever the practical one, simply told him to acquire another one. Wes had his reasons for needing the Cat excavator, and Fergus was fine with it. He trusted Wes's judgment and knew the task was important, whatever it may be.

Wes had already marked out the excavation area for his project and set to work, carefully digging into the decomposed granite. After some time, he had reached a depth of about half a meter, and he began piling the removed material nearby for later backfilling. But then, as he continued digging, the ground beneath him changed unexpectedly. The decomposed granite shifted to a lighter-coloured clay, which Wes knew would be less useful for his excavation project.

Without hesitation, he began loading the clay material onto the tipper truck, intending to take it to the landfill area near the camp. This was the same spot that had been used as a rubbish tip for the camp, the 'Gatehouse,' and now, the house at StezPark. While it may have seemed like a simple disposal task, Wes's decision to take the clay to the landfill area was thoughtful. He wasn't just dumping it, it was also helping to improve the aesthetics of the site, especially with all the waste piling up there.

Tim, who had noticed the work Wes was putting in, found himself somewhat puzzled. It wasn't the first time he had seen Wes go to extra lengths for a seemingly small task, but this particular one left him wondering. Why go to all this trouble with the landfill? Why cover the refuse with clay when it didn't seem strictly necessary? He couldn't quite figure it out, but he had to admit that the results were noticeable. The landfill area looked cleaner, tidier, and far more manageable, and most importantly, it seemed to keep Wes busy and entertained.

The fact that Wes was so focused on the task, and not distracted by other matters, gave Tim a bit of peace of mind. It was clear that Wes enjoyed the work he was doing, no matter how mundane it might have seemed to an outsider. And in the end, keeping Wes engaged was probably the most important thing. It meant that things were getting done, and without causing any unnecessary disruptions.

One evening, as Fergus took a casual pool shot, he asked Wes with mild curiosity, "What's the idea behind covering the garbage over at the landfill? Not that I don't think it looks good, just curious."

Wes didn't even pause his focus on the game, answering as if it were the most natural thing in the world, "Well, if one is searching for something that seems to have disappeared and comes upon a large pile of earth, then it may seem suspicious."

Fergus blinked, taken aback by the thoughtfulness of the answer. Once again, he found himself amazed at Wes's calculated precision. It was clear to him now: Wes wasn't just going through the motions. Everything he did had purpose, and this was no exception. The more Fergus thought about it, the more he became convinced that Wes's plan was almost complete, and that it would most likely succeed. The sergeant, or possibly both of them, might never be found, their disappearances buried beneath layers of thought-out actions, all unnoticed and concealed with meticulous care.

The conversation shifted in his mind as he reflected on the new development in Mitchell's life.

Mitchell had recently turned eighteen, marking a significant turning point in his life. During his time at Stezland, he had worked tirelessly to ensure the property ran smoothly and that Stezland Pastoral Pty Ltd's interests were safeguarded. However, with the middle of December approaching and the wet season about to start, his duties checking the bores and overseeing the cattle yards and enclosures would soon be on hold. The shift in the season was an unavoidable change, meaning Mitchell could finally start focusing on the future.

Having enrolled at James Cook University for a Bachelor of Veterinary Science, Mitchell was set to begin his studies at the Townsville campus and at Fletcherview Station, situated west of Townsville. The five-year full-time program would mark the next chapter of his life, one that took him away from Stezland, even though he could still return regularly, it was only a six hundred-kilometre drive.

He would miss the familiarity of Stezland, the place that had been his world for so long, but this was his time to step into a new role, with new responsibilities and opportunities. Now that he was eighteen, he was allowed to take his Landcruiser off the property. Eager to make the most of the independence this brought, Mitchell decided to drive into Cooktown. He'd told Bian of his plans, and as was typical, she handed him a list of things to pick up while he was there. His casual offer to help out had led to this, and though he found it slightly annoying, he obliged, not wanting to make a fuss over a few errands.

The midday sun was already relentless, casting a shimmering haze over the landscape as Mitchell made his way along the familiar route. The temperature was rising, promising an even hotter day as he passed the camp and waved to Ken at the 'Gatehouse'. Further along, he waved to Rodney and Jason. It was just after twelve o'clock when he crossed the newly completed causeway, the steady rumble of the Landcruiser's tires offering a rhythmic accompaniment to his thoughts.

The Aftermath

It was a scorching 35°C, and with the oppressive heat making it unbearable to be outside, Fergus and Wes had just returned from the bull sales at Mareeba. They had finished lunch and were relaxing at the bar in the snooker room when Mitchell walked in, his face drawn with distress. Without a word, he rushed over and embraced Fergus, shaking as he began to sob uncontrollably.

"Dad! Dad... I've fucked up big time," Mitchell choked out, his voice thick with panic.

Wes, who had been lounging in his seat, stood up instinctively, preparing to leave. But Mitchell, still clinging to his father, looked up through his tears and said, "Wes, don't go... just listen first."

Mitchell had always found a sense of security and safety in Wes's presence, and now, in the face of his own unraveling, he felt he needed that more than ever.

Slowly, Mitchell composed himself. His breathing was laboured, his hands trembling as he gathered his thoughts. Finally, in a quiet, almost monotonous voice, he began to recount what had just transpired in Cooktown.

Wes and Fergus sat in complete silence, listening intently. For reasons he couldn't quite place, Fergus found himself skeptical, unable to fully grasp what Mitchell was saying. It all sounded... off, somehow. His instincts told him this might be some sort of dramatic exaggeration, but his son's distress was undeniable. They all sat there, looking at one another in stunned silence for what felt like an eternity.

Then, almost in unison, both Fergus and Wes asked the same question: "You've killed both of the police sergeants?"

Mitchell's face crumpled with anguish. "I don't know if they're dead! I only shot them once each... I only shot all of them once... Oh, fuck me... what have I done? Please help me, Dad. I'm so sorry. I don't know what to do now. What should I do?"

Fergus's face tightened as he cut Mitchell off. "Getting upset is not going to help anything. Calm down. Have another drink and tell us again, slowly, what happened."

Mitchell did just that. He repeated his story, almost word for word, more than three times. His responses never wavered, never changed. The tale seemed incredible, a wild cascade of bad decisions and worse timing. What could have driven him to this point? Both Wes and Fergus probed with more questions, trying to unravel the tangled web of events.

The answers came slowly, but they weren't enough. The real question hanging in the air was simple: were the sergeants dead, or not? As much as they wanted to know, Fergus and Wes soon realised that it didn't matter. Whether the two men were alive or dead, Mitchell had still put himself in a position from which there was no easy escape.

The more they discussed it, the more the details seemed to fall into place.

"You fired how many shots?" Wes asked, his gaze narrowing.

"Five," Mitchell answered, pulling four empty .30-30 cartridge cases from his pocket. "There's another one in the chamber. There were only five in the rifle. If I'd missed with the last shot, he would've got me."

Mitchell's composure had improved somewhat, but his mind was still racing, struggling to make sense of what he had done. As he spoke, Wes's expression softened with reluctant admiration. For all the chaos and terror of the situation, Mitchell had remained focused enough to take down five men with five shots. A .30-30 lever-action rifle wasn't known for its precision, but Mitchell had somehow made it work. In Wes's eyes, this was a moment of surprising skill under extreme pressure.

As the afternoon wore on, the grilling continued. Fergus and Wes asked more questions, but nothing shifted the core of the story. The tension in the room was palpable, but then Mitchell suddenly blurted out something unexpected.

"I came in by the back gate."

Fergus sprang to his feet, his heart racing. "Did you have the air conditioning on in your cruiser when you left here?" he demanded.

Mitchell nodded. "Yeah, it was so hot."

Fergus's eyes sharpened. "So, your windows were up when you left... quickly. We need to report that your car's been stolen. Do it now, quickly!"

Wes, on the same wavelength, added urgently, "Hurry. Call now."

Fergus was already at the bar, rifling through the telephone book. "Here it is!" he called out, as Mitchell dialled the number and added, "Stay calm. Talk slowly."

But there was no answer from the Cooktown police. They tried again, but the line rang out.

Fergus's mind was racing. He quickly found the number for the Mareeba police station. "Try this," he said, passing the number to Mitchell.

"Can I report a stolen vehicle?" Mitchell's voice was steady as he spoke to the officer who answered. "It was stolen from our property near Shiptons Flat... Yes, near Cooktown. Mitchell Laird. The property is Stezland, on the unnamed creek road... Just now, I went outside and it's gone. Okay... our number is..."

Mitchell recounted the officer's response. The Cooktown police were too busy at the moment, but the constable would pass the information along.

Fergus exchanged a look with Wes. "Put his car in your hole, Wes," he said, his tone grave.

Turning to Mitchell, Fergus gave a firm command. "Where's your rifle?"

"It's under the seat, Dad."

"Good. It stays there. I'll follow you up with the Komatsu loader. Mitchell, stay here. Don't answer the phone if it rings. Tell Bian you didn't go to town today because your car was missing, but don't say too much to anyone. Understand?"

Mitchell nodded, still shaken but beginning to follow his father's instructions. As Fergus left the room, the weight of the situation bore down on them all. They were on the verge of a decision that could change everything.

The excavation was about three meters deep, with a steep ramp that would allow a vehicle to descend, but there was no way it could ascend again, in accordance with the design. Wes drove Mitchell's relatively new Landcruiser, worth over fifty thousand dollars, down into the hole. As he climbed back up the steep ramp to the quarry floor, Fergus arrived with the Komatsu articulated front-end loader. The sound of the massive machine filled the air as it began to fill in Wes's carefully excavated hole. After about fifteen minutes, the ground was level again, and no one would ever know what lay buried beneath the quarry floor.

The story they would tell was simple and neat: Mitchell had accompanied his father and Wes to the Mareeba Bull Sales that morning, returning home around two o'clock that afternoon. He had planned to drive into Cooktown shortly thereafter to pick up some things for Bian, but when he went to retrieve his car at around two-thirty, it was gone. He reported it stolen to the police by 2:40 p.m.

Later, the three of them moved a small herd of bullocks from the camp paddocks into the paddock behind the house. This was done strategically, to cover any potential tire tracks leading from the creek and away from the scene.

That evening, Fergus drove down to the camp to see Ken. He told Ken that Mitchell's car had been stolen while they were away at the bull markets in Mareeba. Ken recalled seeing the cruiser around midday but couldn't be sure it was Mitchell driving, as the windows were rolled up and the glare made it hard to tell. He had just assumed it was Mitchell.

Next, Fergus visited Rodney, who also recalled seeing a vehicle that could have been Mitchell's. He and Jason had waved, thinking it was him, but they weren't sure.

At dinner, the conversation was intentionally light, avoiding any mention of the events of the day. They acted casual, hoping to maintain a sense of normalcy and not alert the Vietnamese staff to anything amiss. After dinner, they moved to the snooker room, and the tone of the conversation changed dramatically.

"You have to realize, Mitchell, that if the police discover it was you at the pub today who shot those people, whether they're dead or not, you will go to prison for life," Fergus said, his voice firm but calm. "Your whole life will be ruined, and I'm not going to let that happen. Neither is Wes. If you follow our lead, stay calm, and play it cool, then you might escape going to prison. But it'll be a lie, a very big lie, and you can never tell anyone the truth. Do you understand?"

Mitchell's face twisted with guilt. "But I don't think I can live with myself, Dad, after what I did," he said, his voice breaking. "I can't just pretend it didn't happen."

Fergus's gaze softened but remained steady. "It doesn't matter how you feel. Guilt doesn't help. If you're out of prison, you might be able to get over it. If you're in prison, you'll never escape it, and it won't change anything. Sure, you've made a huge mistake, but prison isn't going to fix what you've done. You'll never forget it, Mitchell, if you're locked away. But we'll help you get through it," he added.

Wes nodded in agreement. "You'll never forget what happened, but we'll make sure you can keep moving forward," he said quietly.

The decision was made. They would all move forward as if they knew nothing other than the supposed theft of Mitchell's car.

Just then, there was a knock at the snooker room door. They always kept it closed when they were inside, as the language could get colourful at times.

"Yes?" called Fergus.

Bian's head poked around the door. "Misters need anything more for evening? I going bed," she said, her broken English endearing.

"No, we're fine. Thank you, Bian. Goodnight," Fergus replied.

"Okay, night... You hear news of big shooting at Cooktown today?" Bian asked, pushing the door open a little wider.

Fergus feigned surprise. "No, what news, Bian? Come in and tell me, please," he said, gesturing for her to enter.

Bian entered and, in her limited English, explained that five people had been shot dead in a hotel bar in Cooktown that afternoon. The police were blocking all roads in and out of the town and were conducting searches. She added that it was fortunate Mitchell had not gone to town that day.

They all reacted with shock and disbelief, even though they had already known the full story. Once Bian left, they gathered more drinks and Wes muttered, "It begins."

Fergus exchanged a glance with Wes. He realised both of them were wearing the bright green "Cattleman" shirts with the Stezland Pastoral logo embroidered above the left pocket. Fergus had bought three of these shirts for each of them, and now, a sudden thought struck him. He rushed to his bedroom and returned with one of the other "Cattleman" shirts, handing it to Mitchell.

"Wear this tomorrow and every day until I can get you some of your size," Fergus instructed. "If anyone asks, it's what you've been wearing every day this week. You've been working up at the yards, and no one has seen you. No one will know."

Wes offered to give one of his shirts to Mitchell as well, but Fergus quickly dismissed the idea. "You haven't been to Cooktown in at least two years, Mitch. It's unlikely anyone would recognise you, and even if they did, they'd just describe a khaki shirt."

With that settled, all they could do was wait and see what unfolded in the coming days.

Wes mixed Mitchell a stiff schnapps and Coke, urging him to drink it along with a couple of homebrew beers so he could sleep through the night without nightmares.

Fergus made plans to visit the camp office in the morning on the pretence of checking in with Tim about some business. He would see if any news had come in from workers who lived in Cooktown.

No one, other than the Vietnamese staff, slept that night. Fergus woke up just before midnight, unable to fall back asleep. He dressed and made his way to the snooker room for a drink, only to find Wes and Mitchell still awake, playing pool, their faces tense but trying to keep their minds off what had happened.

The next morning, the camp was buzzing with news about the shootings in Cooktown. The details were still unclear and mostly second-hand, but the word was that the police were looking for a white Landcruiser driven by a slim man, though there was no concrete description of the suspect. What was known, however, was that the man had shot and killed five people in the pub, including two police officers.

"Fuck," Fergus muttered to Tim and anyone else who could hear. "Might have been the prick who stole Mitch's ute yesterday morning."

One of the plant operators, who had heard the news, chimed in from across the camp. "Could be the same bastard who shot those poor cunts in the pub! You better tell the coppers, boss!"

Fergus nodded grimly, his thoughts already racing. "Yeah, we tried calling yesterday, but no one answered the phone. I think I'd better go into town and see them myself."

With a plan forming in his mind, Fergus went back to the house. He found Mitchell and told him, "I'm going into Cooktown with you. Best thing we can do now is have you front up to report your stolen car. You'll need to look angry at first, but totally shocked if they tell you that your car might've been taken by the same person they're looking for."

Mitchell looked hesitant, still shaken by the events of the day before. But Fergus reassured him. "It'll be fine. Just act like you're supposed to, and they'll buy it."

Fergus then called out to Wes, who was still in bed. "You want to come into town, Wes?"

Wes groggily responded, "Yeah, I'll come. Not much else to do."

The three of them climbed into the Land Rover, and they headed toward Cooktown. Just as they crossed the bridge at Shiptons Flat, they noticed a police car parked in the incoming lane, with two officers standing beside it. Fergus slowed as they approached, rolling down the window and asking one of the officers, "What's going on?"

The officer glanced up, his gaze hard but professional. "Just checking all vehicles coming from the North."

"Any particular reason?" Fergus asked, his curiosity piqued.

The officer raised an eyebrow. "You haven't heard the news?"

"Some of the workers were talking about a shooting at the Cooktown Pub last night," Fergus offered, trying to keep things casual.

"A bit more than that," the officer said, lowering his voice slightly. "But if you're heading to Cooktown, you'll probably hear all about it."

"Yeah, we're on our way to report a vehicle theft from our property yesterday morning," Fergus said, keeping his tone steady.

"Pull over there, please, sir," the other officer, a senior constable, instructed.

Fergus complied, bringing the Land Rover to a stop. He glanced at Mitchell in the back seat, who was holding up surprisingly well, though his face betrayed his unease.

Fergus filled out a full report for the constables, providing a detailed description of the stolen vehicle, including its last known location. Once he finished, the senior constable nodded and said, "There's no need for you to go into Cooktown. We'll handle the report here. The detectives may want to speak to you later."

"That suits us," Fergus replied, trying to sound nonchalant. "We're flat out trying to get organised before the wet season, and now we're a vehicle down."

The constable nodded and handed the paperwork back to Fergus. After a quick three-point turn, they headed back to the camp, their minds spinning with the implications of everything they'd just learned.

When they arrived back at the camp, Tim was already waiting for them in the office, his expression grim.

"That mongrel Sutton was killed in the shooting yesterday," Tim said, his voice low.

Fergus froze. He hadn't expected that news, and it hit him harder than he anticipated. His gut twisted with shock, and Wes's face turned pale, the news clearly striking him just as hard.

Tim continued, filling in more details. "Some other police sergeant got shot too, but I don't know his name. Thought there was only one sergeant at the Cooktown Police Station. Also, three Aborigines were killed, but two of them were from out of town, Kalkadoon's from Mount Isa, apparently."

The gravity of the situation was beginning to settle in. The confusion of the morning's events had now turned into something far more serious.

Fergus stood motionless for a moment, trying to process everything. The shooting had escalated in a way they hadn't expected, and the police were already connecting dots that could bring unwanted attention back to them.

"What now?" Wes asked, his voice quiet but filled with a sense of unease.

Fergus didn't have an immediate answer. All he could do was focus on managing the situation and keeping Mitchell out of the spotlight. The less anyone knew, the better. The consequences of this chain of events were only just starting to unfold, and no one knew how deep it would go.

Tim had just finished giving an update on the situation. "No one seems to know who the white guy was," he said, shaking his head. "He hasn't been seen around Cooktown before, but a few people mentioned they saw his truck. Said it looked like a new Landcruiser ute."

The men had left the camp office and were heading back to the house for breakfast when Wes, almost absentmindedly, muttered, "Bet it was fucking Kirkland."

Fergus nodded thoughtfully. "That's exactly what I was thinking." Then, turning to Mitchell, he asked, "Mitchell, did one of those coppers from yesterday look like the guy you think killed your mum?"

Mitchell's face tightened, the weight of the question clearly bothering him. He swallowed hard before replying. "Dad, I only saw cops who were shooting at me... they were trying to kill me. I honestly don't know what they looked like other than police firing their guns at me, and I just knew that if I didn't kill them, they were going to kill me."

His voice faltered midway through the confession, and for a moment, he seemed as if he might collapse under the strain of his emotions. Fergus placed a reassuring hand on his son's shoulder, trying to calm him.

"It's OK, son," Fergus said softly, his voice steady. "Let it go. Don't worry. Remember, you've got to stay strong... OK?"

Mitchell nodded, his eyes red-rimmed but resolute.

The house had barely settled back into a moment of calm when the phone rang. Fergus answered quickly, and it was Tim on the other end. "Expect company soon," Tim said, his voice low. "Two plainclothes cops are heading your way."

Fergus thanked him and hung up the phone. As soon as he did, it rang again. This time, it was Rodney. "Looks like 'D' is coming down to see us," Rodney said, and then added, "Did you hear the news?"

Fergus sighed, rubbing his temples in frustration. "Yeah, bits and pieces. The cops are probably coming about Mitch's stolen ute."

"Well, don't be surprised if they ask a few more questions," Rodney replied, his tone cautious.

Fergus hung up and exchanged a look with Wes. The weight of what was happening, what Mitchell had done, the unfolding consequences, was becoming more and more real with each passing hour.

"Looks like we're about to have company," Fergus muttered, trying to keep his mind focused.

As they walked back to the house to prepare for the officers' arrival, the tension hung in the air. The quiet of the morning had been shattered, and now, the fear of what might come next loomed over them all.

Fergus opened the door to the police, allowing them into the lounge where Mitchell and Wes were already waiting. The two detectives introduced themselves with a formal air, and Fergus, maintaining his usual calm demeanour, asked the question on his mind.

"Is this about Mitchell's missing ute?" he asked, casually leaning against the doorframe.

The senior detective, an older man with a stern expression, didn't waste any time with pleasantries. "The first thing we need from you is to tell us where you all were yesterday between noon and two o'clock."

Fergus didn't hesitate. "We were on our way back from Mareeba, from the Bull Sales," he said flatly. He glanced at Mitchell before continuing, "Mitchell didn't realise his ute was missing until around two-thirty, give or take."

The detective's gaze sharpened as he turned to Fergus. "We're not talking about the ute, Mr. Laird. Can you prove you were in Mareeba yesterday, and at what time?"

Fergus's calm was starting to crack, but he didn't let it show. He remained composed, thinking quickly. "I have the receipts for four bulls, though, of course, it won't show the exact time, just the date." He paused, then remembered something important. "When we had smoko yesterday in Mareeba, we both had fish and chips and Wes had a burger. I paid for the three meals on my credit card."

Fergus's voice brightened with the realisation. "I still have the receipt from yesterday, it's probably still in my shirt pocket." He left the room for a moment, then returned with the crumpled receipt, the time stamped clearly on it, 10:46 AM.

The detective took the receipt without a word and began flipping through it. "That's fine," he muttered. "Now, about Mitchell's ute, was it locked?"

"No," Mitchell answered, his voice tense.

"Were the keys inside?" the detective asked, not looking up.

"Yes," Mitchell replied, a note of frustration creeping into his tone.

The detective didn't let up. "What else was in the ute?"

"Handheld GPS, a two-way handheld radio, a machete, an Akubra hat, and a rifle," Mitchell responded, each item rolling off his tongue with the kind of memory someone might have under stress.

At the mention of the rifle, the senior detective's expression stiffened, his attention sharpening. He leaned forward. "What kind of rifle?"

"30-30 Winchester," Mitchell said.

"Was it loaded?"

"Yes, five rounds."

"Any more ammo in the car?"

"No, just an empty box in the glove box, I think."

The detective scribbled some notes before asking, "When did you report the vehicle stolen?"

"About... three o'clock," Mitchell answered hesitantly.

"And to whom?"

"I tried calling the Cooktown Police Station, but no one answered, so I called Mareeba. They told me to come report it in person to Cooktown today, this morning."

Fergus interjected at that moment, his voice steady. "We left to go into Cooktown this morning, and we met the police at the roadblock. They took the details of the stolen vehicle and then we came straight back here."

The detectives absorbed the information quietly. After a moment, the senior detective looked at Mitchell with a grim expression. "You'll be reprimanded for not locking your vehicle and not securing your weapon, but that'll be the extent of it. It's a lesson learned." He leaned closer and lowered his voice, as if sharing a secret. "Don't take this as official advice, but when you file an insurance claim, make sure you tell them the ute was locked. They rarely read the police report in detail, and if they know the vehicle was unlocked, those thieving pricks will cancel your insurance without hesitation."

The detective paused for a moment, his face softening just slightly. "Good luck, mate."

And just like that, the detectives turned and left, leaving behind a lingering sense of unease.

Fergus let out a slow breath, his thoughts a whirlwind. Mitchell sat stiffly in his chair, his face pale but composed.

Wes, who had remained quiet throughout, exchanged a brief glance with Fergus. They all knew they had just narrowly escaped the sharp scrutiny of the police, and for now, that was a small victory in the larger, more dangerous game they were playing.

Epilogue

Mitchell filed a claim with his comprehensive insurance company for the stolen ute. Given that the vehicle was under two years old, it was eligible for a full replacement, and the process went relatively smoothly. However, things took a turn when Mitchell received a reprimand from the Firearms Licensing Police. His firearm license was suspended for one year, a consequence that stung, though it didn't come as a complete surprise.

The deaths of the two police sergeants went largely unnoticed in the grand scheme of things. The funerals were low-key affairs, attended only by a handful of people, with no outpouring of public grief. For Wes, Fergus, and Tim, and many other locals, the passing of the officers felt like little more than a shadow in the corner of a long and troubled history. The two men had left little behind in terms of a legacy, and their absence was hardly felt.

The local Aboriginal man who had been tragically shot by accident was remembered with sadness by his family and his community. While his loss was deeply felt, there was no anger directed toward the unknown white man who had fired the fatal shot. The general consensus within the community was that the true blame lay with the visiting Kalkadoon men, outsiders known for stirring trouble. It was their actions that had ignited the chain of events leading to the violence, and in the end, the focus was on the grief of the family rather than any hatred or vendetta.

As for the Cooktown shootings themselves, they remained unsolved. Despite the investigation and the intense scrutiny, no one had been charged, and the case seemed to fade into the background of local life. The lingering sense of unease remained, but life, as it often does, moved on.

In the end, the impact of that tragic day was felt in quiet, invisible ways, affecting the lives of those involved but leaving no tangible closure. The streets of Cooktown carried on, the memory of the shootings slipping slowly into the folds of history, unanswered and unresolved.

End.......

Did you enjoy this book?...

If so please tell your friends and I would appreciate it greatly if you could rate it.

Thanks! ... Max

The New March

Max Barrington

Other Books By Max Barrington

Woolgar River Park

Task

Dying To Find Gold

Harry Croft

The New March

Bad Company

The First Ten Years in Australia

Fifty Five More Years

The Writer & The Written

What's Mine is Yours

The Darkie's Gold

The Intrusion

www.ingramcontent.com/pod-product-compliance
Lightning Source LLC
Chambersburg PA
CBHW030528010526
44110CB00048B/776